Lifeboat Design and Development No.10

THAMES
FAST AFLOAT LIFEBOATS

The RNLI's Thames class lifeboats, their design, history and careers

Nicholas Leach
FOXGLOVE PUBLISHING

First published 2024

Published by
Foxglove Publishing Ltd
Foxglove House, Shute Hill,
Lichfield WS13 8DB
United Kingdom
Tel 07940 905046

© Nicholas Leach 2024

The right of the Author to be identified as the Author of this work has been asserted in accordance with the Copyrights, Designs and Patents Act 1988.

All rights reserved. No part of this book may be reprinted or reproduced or utilised in any form or by any electronic, mechanical or other means, now known or hereafter invented, including photocopying and recording, or in any information storage or retrieval system, without the permission in writing from the Publishers. British Library Cataloguing in Publication Data.

ISBN 9781909540309

Typesetting/layout by
Nicholas Leach/
Foxglove Publishing

LIFEBOAT BOOKS FROM FOXGLOVE PUBLISHING

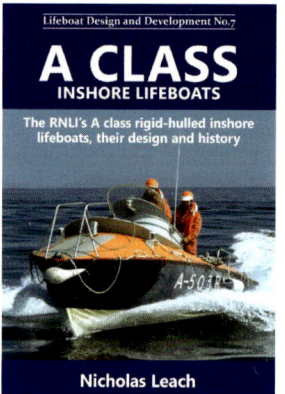
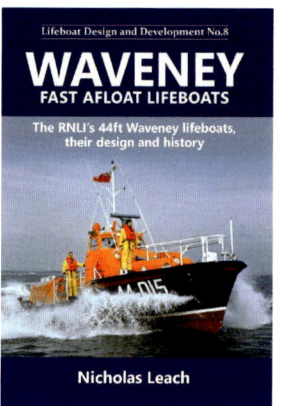

AVAILABLE ONLINE • FOXGLOVE-PUBLISHING.COMPANY.SITE

LIFEBOAT DESIGN AND DEVELOPMENT SERIES This is the tenth book in a series of illustrated volumes that trace the history of and describe technical aspects of RNLI motor lifeboat types. The other volumes in the series are: No.1 Clyde class rescue cruisers; No.2 Surf motor lifeboats, of which ten were built; No.3 Atlantic rigid-inflatable inshore lifeboats; No.4 47ft Tyne fast slipway lifeboats; No.5 60ft Barnett twin-screw motor lifeboats, of which four were built; No.6 33ft Brede intermediate lifeboats; No.7 A class rigid-hulled inshore lifeboats; No.8 Waveney fast afloat lifeboats; and No.9 Steam lifeboats.

THE AUTHOR Nicholas Leach has a long-standing interest in lifeboats and the lifeboat service. He has written many articles, books and papers on the subject, including a history of the origins of the lifeboat service; a comprehensive record of the RNLI's lifeboat stations in 1999, the organisation's 175th anniversary; RNLI Motor Lifeboats, a detailed history of the development of powered lifeboats; and numerous station histories, including ones covering the stations of Cromer, Longhope, Padstow, Sennen Cove, Weymouth and Humber. He has visited all of the lifeboat stations in the UK and Ireland, past and present, and is Editor of Ships Monthly, the international shipping magazine, and Lifeboats Past & Present, the magazine for lifeboat enthusiasts.

Contents

Introduction	5
The introduction of fast lifeboats	7
The Thames design	13
Rotary Service	37
Helmut Schroder of Dunlossit	59
After service	71
Postscript	84
Gore Point	90
Map	92

Acknowledgements

This publication has drawn on the knowledge of Scott Snowling, undoubted expert on the Thames class lifeboats in general and the first, Rotary Service, in particular. Hayley Whiting of the RNLI Heritage Trust provided research facilities and supplied documents relating to the development of the Thames. Former RNLI Operations Director Michael Vlasto kindly shared his experience with 50-002 at Islay. Simon Culliford, at Falmouth, provided images and information about 50-001 in Cornwall. In New Zealand, Alan Calvert and Victor H. Young have been of much help. Mike Louagie kindly allowed use of his photographs. And Ian Moignard thoroughly proofed the text as only he can. I am very grateful to them all.

Nicholas Leach, Lichfield, February 2024

Bibliography

Anon (1973): Suffolk firm building faster boats for the RNLI (The Lifeboat, Vol.XLIII, No.444, Summer, pp.19-21).

Davies, Joan (1974): Trials for two (The Lifeboat, Vol.XLIII, No.448, Summer, pp.166-167).

— (1974): International Lifeboat Exhibition (The Lifeboat, Vol.XLIII, No.449, Autumn, pp.208-212).

Leach, Nicholas (2005): RNLI Motor Lifeboats (Landmark Publishing Limited, Ashbourne).

— (2019): Powering to the Rescue (Lily Publications, Ramsey Isle of Man).

Morris, Jeff (1998): The Story of the Dover Lifeboats (3rd edition).

Summary of Thames class lifeboats

ON	Year (Yard no) Builder	Len Bre	Name Donor	Stations (launches/lives saved) Disposal
1031	1973 (B 394) Brooke Marine Lowestoft	50' 14'6"	**Rotary Service** Rotary International, Great Britain & Ireland; plus legacies of Mr D.I. Craig, Miss Mary Ann Redgate and Miss Mary Coubrough Fowkes.	Falmouth 12.1974–1978 (45/17) Dover 10.1979 – 3.1997 (454/200) Sold 17.6.1998
1032	1974 (B 395) Brooke Marine Lowestoft	50' 14'6"	**Elizabeth Ann/** 1979- **Helmut Schroder of Dunlossit** Appropriated to the gift provided by the Schroder Charity Trust on behalf of Mr Bruno Schroder and Mrs George Mallinckrodt, plus RNLI funds.	Islay 5.1979 – 2.1997 (210/60) Sold 23.6.1998

Engines Twin 390hp General Motors 8V-71TI diesels (8 = number of cylinders, V= V configuration, 71 - volume of each cylinder in cubic centimetres, TI = turbocharged and intercooled)

Introduction

The Thames class was an unusual lifeboat design developed by the Royal National Lifeboat Institution (RNLI) in the early 1970s at a time when the service was looking to build lifeboats which were both faster than the post-1945 designs and had a self-righting capability. Only two examples of the Thames class were completed for operational duties, and they were therefore anomalies in the RNLI fleet. Their development took place at the same time as that of the slightly larger Arun class, but because of the Thames' initial design flaws – which took several years and considerable effort to rectify – the class became sidelined, and the RNLI instead expanded its fleet of 'fast afloat boats' (FAB) by building no fewer than forty-six Arun class lifeboats.

The initial design and development of the Thames took place at Lowestoft in conjunction with Brooke Marine Ltd, who built the boats.

▼ The first Thames class lifeboat on trials out of Lowestoft. (By courtesy of the RNLI)

▲ The 48ft Oakley self-righting lifeboat Earl and Countess Howe (ON.968) was built in 1963 at which time she was regarded as the latest in lifeboat technology, although her hull shape was broadly similar to that of motor lifeboats built half a century earlier. The Thames was a radical departure in terms of speed, hull shape and overall design. (By courtesy of the RNLI)

Subsequent trials and testing showed major flaws in the hull shape, which took several years to resolve, as different bows were fitted to both boats at different times, and the wheelhouse layout was also modified and improved. Eventually, the issues were overcome and the two boats, having been extensively rebuilt in the mid-1970s, entered service. Peculiarly both boats were allocated to Falmouth at some stage in the 1970s, but only 50-001 served there, but only on a temporary basis. Orders for four further Thames boats (50-003 to 50-006) were placed, but cancelled in light of the design difficulties with the first two boats.

In spite of the problems with their initial design and consequent delayed entry into service, both 50-001 and 50-002 gave outstanding service at their stations, respectively Dover and Islay. The former was involved in medal-winning rescues, while the latter capsized on service in horrendous conditions, successfully righting and ensuring the safety of her volunteer crew. The two boats were replaced in the late 1990s by 17m Severn class lifeboats and were then sold out of service. Their subsequent careers are notable: 50-001 went initially to Fowey, and then to south-west Ireland, before returning to her origins at Lowestoft for restoration, but now facing an uncertain future; 50-002 was taken to New Zealand, where she remains to this day.

The introduction of fast lifeboats in Britain

During the 1960s, the RNLI started to introduce faster all-weather lifeboats, starting with a 44ft steel-hulled self-righting type, the first of which was purchased from the United States Coast Guard. The development of the 50ft Thames should be seen in this context. The 44ft lifeboat was a significant step forward for the RNLI on a number of fronts. For the first time, the Institution had acquired a boat not conceived by its own designers, and showed faith in what were radical ideas for a rescue craft, rather than continuing with the tried and trusted designs of post-war Britain. This 44ft boat, numbered 44-001 by the RNLI, was self-righting by virtue of its watertight cabins, faster than conventional displacement-hulled lifeboats then in service, and was completely different from traditional British lifeboat designs. Hitherto, a more cautious approach had been taken with regard to lifeboat development, with new technology shunned in favour of equipment

◀ The ground-breaking 44-footer from the United States Coast Guard, 44-001, had a speed of about fifteen knots, making it faster than contemporary British lifeboats.

▲ The first 44ft Waveney John F. Kennedy (ON.1001) pictured during her trials off Lowestoft following her completion by Brooke Marine.

that was thoroughly proven in RNLI service, so the acquisition of the 44-footer marked the start of a new approach to lifeboat design.

The US-built boat was taken on an extensive tour around the British Isles, visiting as many lifeboat stations as possible so that crews' opinions of the new design could be gauged. The reaction of the lifeboat crews who experienced the boat was so positive that a building programme was soon embarked upon, with six boats being ordered from the Lowestoft shipbuilding firm Brooke Marine Ltd. Given the class name Waveney

▶ Self-righting trial of the first British-built Waveney John F. Kennedy at Brooke Marine, Lowestoft. (By coutesy of the RNLI)

◀ The second Waveney to be built by the RNLI, Khami (ON.1002), being lifted out of the water at Great Yarmouth for her annual hull inspection on 13 September 1977. This excellent photograph clearly shows the propeller and rudder arrangement on the Waveneys. (Supplied by Paul Russell)

◀ 44ft Waveney Louis Marchesi of Round Table (ON.1045) was the nineteenth of the twenty-two Waveneys. She was stationed at Newhaven, where she was replaced by a 52ft Arun in 1985. (By courtesy of the RNLI)

after the river which flows through Lowestoft, the design became the first of the RNLI's modern generation of 'fast' lifeboats. The British-built Waveneys entered service in 1967, the first at Dun Laoghaire to cover Dublin Bay and the busy approaches to Dublin Port, and the second at Great Yarmouth & Gorleston in Norfolk. The Waveney proved to be a highly successful design and the twenty-two boats of the class that were built for the RNLI were well-liked by the crews who operated them. Indeed, many outstanding medal-winning rescues were carried out using Waveneys, and boats of the class remained in service until well into the 1990s (see Lifeboat Design & Development No.8 for a full history of the Waveney design and the boats in service).

As the Waveney proved that cutting-edge technology could be beneficial, and that fast lifeboats' sea-keeping qualities were more than good enough for search and rescue work, the RNLI's technical teams realised that the heavy iron keels and propeller tunnels hitherto regarded as essential elements to motor lifeboat design could be dispensed with in the interests of greater speed. As a result, in the late 1960s RNLI staff began to look at a larger and faster design, which would be able to better meet the changing demands being made on the lifeboat service by an increasing number of services to pleasure craft. The faster the lifeboat, the quicker a casualty could be reached, thus reducing the chances of a situation deteriorating and making a rescue more difficult.

The result was the development of two new classes of lifeboat: a 50ft steel-hulled boat regarded as an upscaled version of the Waveney (later designated the Thames class), and a 52ft type (later designated the Arun class), which was initially built in wood but designed with the intention that glass-reinforced plastic (GRP) would be used for the majority of the build programme to reduce costs and speed up construction.

▶ The prototype 52ft Arun class lifeboat, named Arun (ON.1018), had a cold-moulded timber hull and aluminium alloy superstructure. She was stationed initially at St Peter Port for a year, before going to Barry Dock for twenty-three years, where she was well liked.

Capable of between eighteen and twenty knots, the Arun represented a new direction for lifeboat design. It had a fully enclosed wheelhouse for rescuers and rescued, a flared bow to protect the deck and wheelhouse from spray and a broad beam for stability, and a flying bridge provided an outside steering position with good visibility. Another advance was

◄ Two 52ft Aruns off Guernsey: Sir William Arnold (ON.1025) and George and Olive Turner (ON.1061). (By courtesy of the RNLI)

◄ 14m Trent Betty Huntbatch (ON.1274) on exercise off Hartlepool, where she was placed on station in 2004. The Trent was the RNLI's first all-weather lifeboat design capable of speeds up to twenty-five knots. (Nicholas Leach)

▲ 17m Severn Annette Hutton (ON.1277) heading out of Castletownbere harbour on exercise. The 17m Severn class, of which forty-five entered service, was the successor to the Arun as well as the Thames class lifeboats, and has proved to be an outstanding rescue craft for more than two decades. (Nicholas Leach)

the hull material. After the first three boats had been constructed from cold-moulded wood, the fourth boat was built in GRP. Its advantages were its strength and economy of build, as a mould could be used to manufacture identical hulls at a time when wooden- and steel-hulled boats were becoming increasingly expensive. During the 1970s the Arun proved to be a fine rescue boat, and a major construction programme was embarked upon by the RNLI, which ended in 1990 when the forty-sixth and last Arun was completed and entered service.

The introduction of the Waveney, Thames and Arun classes marked the beginning of the modernisation of the lifeboat fleet. During the 1980s and 1990s the RNLI's quest for faster and safer lifeboats continued, with new even faster new types being introduced. In the early 1980s a large rigid-inflatable design was developed, the Medina, but it never entered operational service, while a smaller 33ft type, the Brede, was developed, based on a commercial GRP hull form and with a top speed of about twenty knots. Then, two twenty-five-knot types were conceived: the 14m Trent and 17m Severn classes, which became the mainstay of the RNLI fleet well into the twenty-first century.

The Thames design

When the RNLI's Committee of Management realised in the early 1970s that, after the successful introduction of the 44ft Waveney, a slightly larger and faster boat was needed, two new designs were produced: the 50ft Thames and the 52ft Arun. RNLI staff undertook the initial design work on the 50ft boat, while a detailed design study was also carried out by Brooke Marine Ltd (builder of the first six Waveneys), and a model was tank-tested by the British Hovercraft Corporation to assess the vessel's performance characteristics. The success of the tests resulted in an order for two boats being placed with Brooke Marine, who had already built a 50ft boat, initially intended as a rescue boat, but which was subsequently used as a pilot boat named Gore Point (see page 90).

▼ 50-001, the first of the Thames class, as built, with her forward superstructure similar to that of the 44ft Waveneys (By courtesy of the RNLI)

50ft steel-hulled lifeboat: technical specifications

The Summer 1973 edition of The Lifeboat magazine contained details of 'the new 50-foot Thames class lifeboats, now being built at Brooke Marine' in an article headed 'Suffolk Firm Building Faster Boats for the RNLI' The article gave the following details:

TECHNICAL DETAILS Length overall 50ft, breadth moulded 14ft 6in, depth moulded 5ft 5in, fuel capacity 400 gallons, drinking water 10 gallons, load displacement 23.5 tons, load draft aft 4ft 6in and for'd 2ft, maximum speed 19 knots, range at full speed 198 nautical miles, cruising speed 17 knots, range at cruising speed 229 nautical miles.

RUDDERS To meet the manoeuvrability requirements twin spade rudders are fitted.

MAIN ENGINES General Motors 8V-71, each developing 390shp at 2,300rpm fitted with Allison hydraulically operated reverse reduction gearboxes giving a reduction of 2:1.

GEARBOXES are handed to give outboard turning propellers. The engines are fitted with single lever engine controls operated from the wheelhouse.

AUXILIARY is a Petter PJ2W diesel which drives both an AC90 generator and a fire and salvage pump.

STARTING The main and auxiliary engines are arranged with electric starting facilities and a 24V DC supply from each of two separate 260 amp hour capacity batteries.

ALTERNATOR Each main engine fitted with a 90 amp alternator.

AUXILIARY SET Fitted with a 90 amp alternator with a Constavolt unit to provide a 24V DC supply for battery charging.

ELECTRICAL SERVICES Lighting throughout, instrumentation, circuit protection and warning systems, ventilation fans, heaters for all working spaces, glow plugs on the main engines for use in cold weather, a windlass and windscreen wipers.

ELECTRONIC EQUIPMENT Kelvin Hughes type 17 W Radar; Decca Navigator Mk.21; Kelvin Hughes Falkland MF radio telephone; Pye Westminster VHF radio transmitter and receiver; Ferrograph echo sounder, and Esco five-station intercom system.

▲ This line drawing was published in The Lifeboat magazine, Summer 1973, page 19, as part of the article describing the new 50ft lifeboat being developed by Brooke Marine.

Although Brooke Marine's pilot boat design was not suitable as a rescue boat, the shipbuilder and the RNLI design team, then based in London, collaborated on another design using elements taken from the pilot boat. The RNLI's basic requirements were for a self-righting boat with an overall length of about 48ft 6in; a speed of about eighteen knots; a radius of action of 100 nautical miles; the draught not to exceed 4ft 9in; a crew of five; and the machinery installation, equipment and navigational aids to conform to RNLI standards. Various options were explored and, after a series of tank tests, changes were made to the initial designs, with the boat's size increased to 50ft overall with a beam of 14ft 6in.

The design was largely based on that of the Waveney, but the hull was 6ft longer and the wheelhouse and chartroom were fully enclosed, with a flying bridge above. The engine room below the wheelhouse was also much larger than that on the Waveney, and the hull plating was of Corten steel. The boat was subdivided by watertight bulkheads into seven compartments: forepeak, anchor cable locker, forecabin, midships cabin, engine-room, after cabin and tiller flat. A double bottom extended from the forepeak to the after engine-room bulkhead. Self-righting was achieved though the boat's inherent buoyancy, which was achieved when the watertight doors to the two cabins were closed.

▼ The first of the Thames class lifeboats, 50-001 under construction at Brooke Marine's shipyard at Lowestoft. The RNLI worked with Brooke Marine on the design for a steel-hulled fast lifeboat.

A first boat, given the operational number 50-001, was ordered from the Lowestoft yard on 27 September 1971 at a contract price of £77,500. This boat was completed early in 1973 and on 4 May 1973 was shown to the press during self-righting trials. Further trials were held on 9 June 1973, and sea trials out of Lowestoft began on 16 June 1973. On 21 June 1973, at a displacement

▲ The design and construction of 50-001 by Brooke Marine was a prestigious project for the Suffolk-based firm, which had adverts produced promoting its work on the new Thames class lifeboat, several of which appeared in The Lifeboat.

▼ 50-001 heading out of Lowestoft during her sea trials in 1973.

◀ 50-001 on trials, probably off Lowestoft, in 1973. During speed trials undertaken on 21 June 1973, 50-001 reached a maximum speed of 18.4 knots, and averaged 16.9 knots on her full speed runs. She was found to turn through 360 degrees about as quickly as the Arun and Waveney. (By courtesy of the RNLI)

of 24.8 tons, 50-001 achieved a speed of 18.13 knots, with the engines running at 2,390rpm. The boat must have been deemed acceptable following these initial trials, as she left Brooke Marine on 27 July 1973 and, as far as can be ascertained, did not return to Lowestoft until she had long been out of RNLI service. However, problems with the hull and other aspects of the design soon became evident.

Over the following years a series of extensive trials with 50-001 were undertaken, while work on a second 50ft lifeboat got under way at Lowestoft. By then, the new type had been designated the Thames class as much of the design work had been carried out at the RNLI's London offices. In the early 1970s the RNLI had introduced a policy of naming lifeboat classes after rivers, such as the Waveney, after the river which flows through Lowestoft. Clyde, Rother and Arun classes soon followed, named after the rivers where the first boats of each type were built.

Having ordered two Thames class boats in January 1973 the RNLI placed contracts for a further four boats, ON.1038 to ON.1041, which were given operational numbers 50-003 to 50-006. The first two were ordered from Brooke Marine, yard numbers SYC 404 and SYC 405 (SYC refers to South Yard craft, as Brooke Marine had yards on both the north and south sides of the river Waveney); the other two were ordered from Richard Dunston, Hessle, near Hull, a well-known boatyard but one which had never previously constructed lifeboats.

▶ Self-righting trial of 50-001 at Lowestoft. (By courtesy of the RNLI)

◀ 50-001 was self-righting through inherent buoyancy, provided that the two watertight doors were closed. (By courtesy of the RNLI)

◀ 50-001 comes upright at the end of her self-righting trials and the water drains away. (By courtesy of the Port of Lowestoft Research Society/ Stanley Earl)

THAMES LIFEBOATS

Brooke Marine of Lowestoft

The Lowestoft boatbuilding firm of Brooke Marine was heavily involved in the design of the Thames class lifeboat, and was also responsible for its construction. The company had been involved in boat construction for almost a century by the time it was contracted by the RNLI to build the first of the 44ft Waveneys. Brooke had constructed boats and small ships for civilian and commercial use, as well as minor warships for the Royal Navy, Royal Navy of Oman, Royal Australian Navy and US Navy.

The company was founded in 1874 as a foundry by John Walter Brooke and expanded into boatbuilding in the early 1900s. Until 1911 the company, which produced engines and motor cars, sub-contracted its boat building operations to another firm in Oulton Broad. In 1911 it opened a shipyard on the north side of Lake Lothing and began to produce its own craft, fitted with engines produced at its Adrian Works. Car production stopped in 1913.

During World War I the company established a munitions factory. Following the war, the shipyard was expanded to produce boats up to 52ft in length. During World War II the company produced and serviced craft for the Royal Navy. In 1940 the company was acquired by Harry Dowsett and renamed Brooke Marine.

In 1954, a new shipyard was built on the south side of Lake Lothing. The first ships produced at the new yard were twenty fishing trawlers for the Russian government. In July 1977 the company was nationalised and became part of British Shipbuilders until a management buy-out in 1985.

In 1987 Brooke Marine closed but the dockyard was bought by a company trading as Brooke Yachts, which continued trading until September 1992. The name and some assets of Brooke Marine were acquired in 2006 by Michael Fenton, who relaunched the business as Brooke Marine Yachts Ltd, which traded until 2009. The shipyard was then purchased by an investment company which now leases many of the original buildings to a range of businesses. There are plans to redevelop the site for residential-led mixed use.

As the trials with the prototype 50-001 commenced, however, the boat was found to have characteristics that made her unacceptable for life-saving operations. The design flaws were evident to RNLI staff during the first trials, and considerable efforts, over the course of several years, were made to remedy them. The problems were numerous, as not only was the initial hull found to be unsuitable, but the wheelhouse layout also needed rethinking.

The problems with the hull centred around poor manoeuvrability, direction keeping and wetness: the steering gear was inadequate, and the boat took on water over the deck while it was at speed. In August 1973 extensions to the rudders were fitted, and during trials on 7 August 1973 the boat's manoeuvrability was found to have improved, with the Chief Inspector of Lifeboats reporting 'the boat answers her helm much more quickly'; however, overall improvements in course keeping were negligible. A further report by the Chief Inspector, dated 22 August 1973, stated that, during trials undertaken two days earlier, 'the bows were being continually knocked around by even the smallest waves and that if this could be prevented directional stability would be improved', and 'in a beam sea the bows continually paid off'.

▼ 50-001 on trials off Lowestoft in her original as-built configuration. The problems with the bow were twofold: how the lifeboat handled, particularly when running down sea, and the amount of spray that was thrown up as the spray rails on the original bow were relatively ineffective. (By courtesy of the RNLI)

THAMES LIFEBOATS

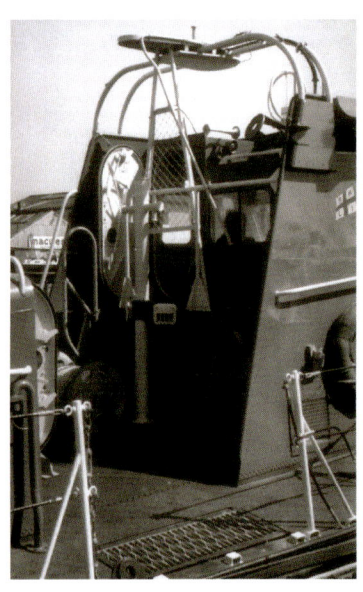

▲ A series of photographs showing 50-001 as she was when first built. She was fitted with a Decca Navigator Mk.21 and a Kelvin Hughes Type 17 W radar, together with other standard electronic equipment. The main engines were twin General Motors 8V-7I diesels, each developing 390bhp at 2,300rpm, fitted with Allison hydraulically operated reverse reduction gearboxes. These gave a cruising speed of seventeen knots and a maximum speed of about nineteen knots. The fuel capacity of 400 gallons meant that, at full speed, the range was almost 200 nautical miles, which increased to 229 nautical miles at cruising speed. However, her electronic fit-out was altered during the course of her service career. (By courtesy of the RNLI)

A complete redesign from scratch was considered, but it was believed this was not needed and 'a deeper forefoot would be beneficial with as little modification as possible to the rest of the underwater form'. The Chief Inspector concluded: 'The boat is comparatively comfortable in a seaway and it is felt that when we solve the problem of directional instability we will have a very useful addition to our fleet.' So plans were made for various bow and hull alterations.

In October 1973 the Chief Staff Officer (Technical) reported further on the problems of the directional stability, which occurred at speeds in excess of twelve knots. With the steering arrangements being queried, a series of modifications were put in hand at the William Osborne Ltd boatyard in Littlehampton. The fitting of a 'bar' keel forward and increasing the depth of rudders resulted in improvements to course keeping and manoeuvrability. On 18 October 1973 the boat was relaunched at Littlehampton having also had a deeper keel fitted forward. Trials carried out in sea states up to 'moderate' showed that course keeping was up to an acceptable operational standard.

Regarding the wheelhouse layout, in November 1973 the Chief Staff Officer (Technical) presented various alternatives, and it was agreed that wheelhouse modifications to both 50-001 and the second boat, designated 50-002 (ON.1032), should be carried out, including an upper steering position being incorporated. Further examination of the wheelhouse layout was also deemed necessary for the other four boats then on order, so that five crew could be seated inside the wheelhouse, while the coxswain's position should also be re-examined. Originally the wheelhouse layout closely followed that of the 44ft Waveney, in which the helmsman was normally the sole occupant; in the Thames class, the wheelhouse was watertight and, in practice, all crew members who sailed on the prototype congregated in the wheelhouse. As a result, it needed to be larger and the layout changed to increase the space.

In March 1974 50-001 was taken to Guernsey, in the Channel Islands, for a series of trials running alongside Sir William Arnold (ON.1025), the second of the 52ft Arun class lifeboats, which had been placed in service at St Peter Port in November 1973 and was found to be an excellent lifeboat. The 52ft Arun, designed by Allen McLachlan, of G. L. Watson, Glasgow, was a broad-beamed wooden-hulled boat with flared bow sections, wide

▶ Trials for two off Guernsey: on parallel courses about 100 yards apart, Arun 52-02 and Thames 50-001 drive through rough seas at a speed of about seventeen knots. Former St Peter Port Coxswain Buz White recalled: 'To start with they [the Thames class boats] were so wet that you could not see out of the windscreen, and on the upper steering position you got soaked. They were taken back to the yard to put a new bow on, which did improve them a little bit'. (Guernsey Evening Press, by courtesy of the RNLI)

decks, broad stern and a spacious wheelhouse. In comparison, 50-001 with her steel hull, was a narrower-beamed boat (14ft compared to 17ft), had straighter bow sections and a tug-type tumblehome, a smaller wheelhouse and an entirely different general arrangement.

RNLI technical staff, together with members of the British Ship Research Association (BSRA), were keen to know what impact rough seas would have on a hull driven at speed by high-powered engines, as well as assess what the strain would be on the propeller shafts and the physical stresses imposed on crews in such a boat.

The trials, run under the supervision of Captain J.C. Allez, Harbour Master and RNLI Honorary Secretary at St Peter Port, provided a comparison of what were the RNLI's latest self-righting lifeboats. In overall command was Captain Roy Harding, the RNLI's trials officer. He coxswained first one boat and then the other, backed up by a crew of William Dent (Selsey Coxswain), Ian Johnson and John Ashford, together with George Moore from Littlehampton ILB station. John Petit, Lloyd de Mouilpied and Bill Ogier of St Peter Port each took turns to coxswain the boats, backed up by Eric Pattimore, Chick Robilliard and Ron Munson. From the RNLI technical staff, and acting as co-ordinators, were Symington MacDonald, chief staff officer (technical), and Stuart Welford, research and development officer.

To measure motion in rough water, the BSRA team, led by Christopher Lamb, fitted both lifeboats with instruments which recorded pitch and roll; the torque, or twist, on each propeller shaft, together with the speed at which the engines were running; the athwartship accelerations experienced by the boat, and hence the human body, at three different positions on the boat: bow, stern and the coxswain's position at the wheel; and the vertical accelerations at bow and stern. A description of the trials was included in the Summer 1974 edition of The Lifeboat magazine, which stated that 'a mass of information was accumulated, which is now being analysed by BSRA and the technical department of the RNLI'.

◀ 50-001 arriving at Poole in 1974, probably before she left for Plymouth for the International lifeboat exhibition at Plymouth in July 1974. (Jeff Morris, by courtesy of the RNLI)

◀ 50-001 arriving at Poole in 1974. In this photo, the false bow can clearly be seen. (Jeff Morris, by courtesy of the RNLI)

THAMES LIFEBOATS

▶ 50-001 at Plymouth in July 1974 for the International lifeboat exhibition. (Grahame Farr, by courtesy of the RNLI)

▼ The upper steering position of 50-001. (Grahame Farr, by courtesy of the RNLI)

Details of the trials were given in a report to a meeting of the RNLI's Technical Consultative Committee on 8 October 1974, in which it was stated that: 'in terms of hull response to the seas, there is very little to choose between the two classes in the conditions experienced during the trials'. But two major issues with the Thames class were highlighted, both of which were already known: the wheelhouse layout and deck wetness. The RNLI staff and crew who took part in the trials also stated that the boat was found to perform poorly in certain sea conditions, and confirmed what had been evident in 1973, that the design of the bow made the boat not only very wet but sometimes difficult to steer on a true course.

Plans were consequently drawn up to modify the boat, with the

▼ 50-001 taking part in the International lifeboat exhibition at Plymouth in July 1974. (By courtesy of the RNLI)

▲ 50-001 in attendance at the International lifeboat exhibition at Plymouth in July 1974. (By courtesy of the RNLI)

◄ 50-001 visiting St Katharine Docks, London, possibly in 1974, but exactly when and why she came to London are not known. (Henry 'Joyful' West)

THAMES LIFEBOATS

most significant alteration being the fitting of a new bow. During the spring of 1974 a false bow made from glass-reinforced plastic was laid over the original steel bow, and further trials undertaken. The new bow was in evidence when, during the summer of 1974, 50-001 was one of a number of lifeboats which took part in the celebrations to mark

▶ 50-001 at Plymouth in July 1974. (By courtesy of Robin West)

▶ 50-001 moored alongside the Polish lifeboat Monsun at Plymouth, July 1974. (By courtesy of Robin West)

▲ RNLI lifeboats at Plymouth in July 1974 for the RNLI's 150th anniversary events. The lifeboats are, left to right: 54ft Arun Edward Bridges (Civil Service & Post Office No.37) (ON.1037); 71ft Clyde City of Bristol (ON.1030); 44ft Waveney Augustine Courtauld (ON.1029); 50ft Thames Rotary Service (ON.1031); and 37ft 6in Rother J. Reginald Corah (ON.1023). (By courtesy of Robin West)

the 150th anniversary of the RNLI's founding, which included a major gathering of lifeboats at Plymouth.

As well as 50-001, ten other lifeboats were in attendance, including various foreign lifeboats, notably the German rescue cruiser Arwed Emminghaus, the 15m lifeboat Patron Emile Guyot from France, and the 80ft cruising lifeboat R.S. Platou from Norway. The RNLI was represented by the new 71ft Clyde lifeboat City of Bristol (ON.1030) destined for Clovelly, the 54ft Arun Edward Bridges (the third Arun, ON.1038) destined for Torbay, and the 44ft Waveney Augustine Courtauld (ON.1029), destined for Poole.

The six foreign lifeboats arrived at Poole on 14 July, being escorted through the harbour by the RNLI lifeboats to Poole Quay. It was the first time the Institution welcomed foreign visitors to its then new headquarters in Dorset. On 16 July the flotilla headed west, rounding Portland Bill, and made for Brixham, before undertaking the final leg of the passage the following day to Plymouth, for the International Lifeboat Exhibition. The event was formally opened on 19 July 1974 by HRH Duke of Kent, President of the RNLI, and lasted until 17 August.

During the lifeboats' time at Brixham, the crew of 50-001 were able to welcome the donors on board. Originally the boat was to be named Elizabeth Ann and was allocated to Falmouth, but at some point in 1974 she was given the name Rotary Service, and visited Plymouth as such. Moneys raised by the Rotary Clubs of Britain and Ireland had been used to fund the boat, and members of the Brixham Rotary Club were treated to a trip around Brixham's outer harbour on 16 July 1974 when 50-001 was on her way to Plymouth. However, no formal naming ceremony was held during her time at Falmouth.

Following her stay in Plymouth during the summer, 50-001 underwent further modifications, which encompassed changes to both the bow and wheelhouse layout. The new bow, formulated in September 1974, was intended to reduce the boat's wetness, while a modified wheelhouse layout was deemed to better suit crews' needs. In November 1974 speed trials were undertaken after 50-001 had been fitted with a larger skeg and rudders. On these trials, she reached 16.91 knots at a displacement of 25.4 tons with engines operating at 2,352rpm.

At the same time, the RNLI's Chief Staff Officer (Technical) outlined proposals to implement the recommendations of the Technical Consultative Committee to reduce the wetness issue through hull changes. Carrying out full-scale modifications, it was determined, was more economical than using model testing. The National Physical Laboratory (NPL), a public sector research establishment, was by now involved in attempts to improve the design, and proposed an increase in the length of the hull by up to two feet, thereby fining its entry into the water. These alterations were carried out on the prototype reasonably cheaply, and a false bow, comprising a steel frame with bays for foam filling and sheathed with GRP.

▶ The original wheelhouse and upper steering position on 50-001, pictured on trials at Falmouth. By the time the boat entered service in the late 1970s this arrangement had been changed considerably.

▲ 50-001 being craned back into the water when she was at Falmouth in the mid-1970s. This photograph gives a good indication of the modified bow, and clearly shows the extended skeg and trim wedges aft. (By courtesy of J.A. Prior)

Work continued on 50-002 at Brooke Marine. She was completed in February 1975, but the same seakeeping and wetness problems that had plagued her sistership were experienced. So she, too, was given the revised NPL-designed bow, as well as being fitted with spray rails to reduce wetness. The existing fore end remained in place, with an experimental false bow, made of rigid foam covered by GRP, being built up over the steel hull forward, to give a finer entry. In April 1975 a quotation from Brooke Marine for the completion of 50-002, including the modifications, was found to be within the estimated budget, and the Boat Committee recommended the incorporation of the larger wheelhouse on the boat.

Meanwhile, 50-001 was sent to Falmouth, the Cornish station for which she had been intended, for operational trials, but she was not well liked by the Falmouth crew. At the RNLI's Technical Consultative Committee meeting of 9 January 1975, it was reported that, after crew training had been completed, 'the unofficial comments from the station were not very encouraging... [but] it was felt [presumably by the RNLI's designers] that fair comment could not be expected until 50-001 had had some experience in service'. Although the boat was not well liked

THAMES LIFEBOATS

▲ 50-001 makes an impressive sight in 1975 during her time at Falmouth, where she was on operational trials during the late 1970s. (David Trotter, by courtesy of the RNLI) ▶

at Falmouth, certainly not initially, her operational time there lasted for almost four years, during which she undertook many rescues.

The continuing problems with the design proved to be both costly and difficult to resolve. Consequently, in June 1975 the orders for the four additional boats were cancelled, with the vessels never having been allocated stations. By then, the Arun class was deemed to be a better boat and was found to be easier to build. The price of steel had increased and the Arun, which was (after the first three wooden-hulled boats) built of glass reinforced plastic, performed better without any significant modifications or alterations being needed. The cancellation came at a financial cost to the RNLI, with £38,000 and £19,000 paid to the two yards, Brooke Marine and Dunston respectively, but against which materials valued at £19,000 became available to the RNLI.

Meanwhile, work continued to try to resolve the ongoing issues with the existing boats. The altered bow fitted to and trialled on 50-002 was found to satisfactorily overcome the wetness problem and, with spray rails also fitted, the craft was deemed acceptable for operational service. A temporary bow of foam and GRP designed by NPL was then also fitted to 50-001, and at last it seemed that the Thames class' hull was going to be suitable for life-saving work. Machinery and speed trials around the coast undertaken in 1976 showed that the issues with 50-002, compared to 50-001, had been mostly overcome and than on her final speed trials she achieved nearly 1.8 knots greater maximum speed than did 50-001, in spite of an increase in her displacement of two and a quarter tons.

◀ 50-002 leaving Lowestoft on trials in the early 1970s. During speed trials undertaken on 8 July 1976, 50-002 reached a maximum speed of 19.9 knots, with a trials displacement of 27.65 tons, and an average top speed of 18.7 knots in calm conditions. (Port of Lowestoft Research Society)

THAMES LIFEBOATS

The boat had been taken on a heavy weather passage from Littlehampton to St Peter Port in November 1976, facing force eight squalls and heavy seas. Some slamming had been experienced, but visibility from the helm's position was deemed good. However, a new foredeck arrangement was required to provide better positioning of the equipment. The wheelhouse was also found to be workable and a considerable improvement on that of 50-001. Use of the crew cabin and engine room in heavy weather was only possible when speed was eased, and it was too wet to get to the aft cabin or use the flying bridge.

The changes to the design incorporated in 50-002 pointed the way forward. So, to make the modifications permanent, three shipbuilders were asked to submit quotes in March 1977. The work involved replacing the temporary bow on ON.1032 with a permanent steel bow, which meant cutting off approximately the forward third of the boat and having a completely new steel bow in its place, and the replacement section was then to be fitted out as accommodation space.

Brooke Marine submitted a price of £69,700; Cubow of Woolwich, who had recently undertook the survey of the Sheerness lifeboat (a 44ft Waveney), quoted £51,626; and Fairey Marine of East Cowes (formerly Groves and Guttridge) quoted £51,576. The cost of an overseer visiting Brooke Marine on two days a week was greater that of visiting Cubow and Fairey Marine. Consequently, the Committee recommended that the quotation submitted by Fairey Marine be accepted. The Boat Committee also agreed that, while both Thames class boats should have their bows modified, no further boats of the class should be built.

The work to permanently modify both boats took place during 1978 and 1979. Between March and June 1978 the modifications to 50-002 were undertaken at Fairey Marine, and the boat was then taken to the RNLI Depot at Poole for evaluation trials during August and September 1978. At this time, the lifeboat was allocated to Falmouth and was given the name Elizabeth Ann; however, the RNLI decided to reallocate her to Islay, on the west coast of Scotland, under the name Helmut Schroder of Dunlossit. The Arun ON.1058 (52-11) was given her original allocation and name (Falmouth and Elizabeth Ann) instead. Between October 1978 and April 1979 50-002 was taken to William Osborne's yard at Littlehampton for further acceptance trials. The boat returned to the

◀ Three photographs of 50-002 at William Osborne's boatyard in January 1977, prior to having her hull rebuilt, and showing the wheelhouse with the upper steering position. (Jeff Morris, by courtesy of the RNLI)

◀ The screen fitted to the upper steering position is that mocked up in timber, after earlier screens had proved ineffective. This one was closer to the crew and spread out further to the sides of the wheelhouse and the goalpost mast, which carried the radar scanner and radio aerials. The flying bridge had been found to be very wet when the boat was steaming at speed in anything above Force 4 with seas ahead of the beam. (Jeff Morris, courtesy of the RNLI)

THAMES LIFEBOATS

▲ The second Thames lifeboat, 50-002, undergoing comparative trials off St Peter Port, Guernsey, astern of the second 52ft Arun, Sir William Arnold (ON.1025). The other Thames, 50-001, was also involved. The information which accompanied the photo in The Lifeboat (Autumn 1976, No.457, p.204) stated that 50-002 was named Elizabeth Ann and explained: 'Although only light to moderate weather conditions were encountered, 50-002 compared well with both of her running mates. The main improvements are a bow modification, which reduces wetness, and a better layout for the crew cabin. Some further small modifications remain to be evaluated in heavy weather after which, all being well, the experimental GRP bow will be replaced by a steel structure.'

RNLI Depot at Poole in early April 1979, the crew from Islay came to Poole for training, and at the end of the month the boat headed for her new station, taking up duties at Port Askaig on 2 May 1979.

The modifications to 50-001 were made permanent in 1978 and on 26 April 1978, at an RNLI Committee of Management meeting, it was decided that, following the completion of the work, she would be reallocated to Dover to replace the 44ft Waveney Faithful Forester (ON.1003). Between June and October 1979 the boat was surveyed at Osborne's yard, and then took up duty in Dover on 3 October 1979. After more than six years undergoing modifications, rebuilding, testing, redesigning and evaluation, the two Thames class lifeboats were at last in the RNLI's operational service.

Rotary Service

After Rotary Service (50-001) had spent more than two years on trials following her completion at Lowestoft, she was sent to Falmouth in December 1974, having undergone various alterations to her bow, the shape of her hull and the wheelhouse layout. At some point during the construction process both Thames class lifeboats had been destined for the Cornish station, where they were to have been named Elizabeth Ann. Following her appearance at the International Lifeboat Exhibition in Plymouth, 50-001 went to Falmouth, where she initially served as relief for the 46ft 9in Watson Lilla Marras, Douglas and Will (ON.928), but was later designated as being on temporary station duty.

▼ Rotary Service on trials in her original configuration.

▶ When Rotary Service was lifted out of the water on 29 July 1975 for hull cleaning, anti-fouling and the replacing of all cathodic protection anodes, the work was done free of charge, Falmouth Docks workmen giving up their lunch hour to see the job through. The operation was arranged by Falmouth honorary secretary, Captain Frank Edwards, with the co-operation of Silley Cox and Co, and A.E. Underwood, managing director Falmouth Docks and Engineering Co; it was organised by Barry Timmins (lifeboat signalman). In the volunteer workforce were Coxswain Arthur West, Second Coxswain/ Mechanic Vivian Pentecost and crew member John Mitchell. While Rotary Service was out of the water both propellers were replaced with new ones. (J.A. Prior)

◀ Rotary Service being craned into the water at Falmouth. By the time this photograph was taken, a third window had been added, on either side, at the aft end of the wheelhouse. When the boat was completed, the wheelhouse had two windows on each side.

The first service call answered by 50-001 at Falmouth took place in the early hours of 17 December 1974, when she was launched in response to a sighting of red flares off St Mawes. The casualty was the fishing vessel Cordive, which had broken adrift from her moorings with just a watchman on board. The lifeboat was quickly on scene and the crew passed a line to the vessel, which was towed back to Falmouth Harbour.

The most notable service undertaken by 50-001 at Falmouth came on the evening of 28 November 1977, when the master of the tug Englishman, which had been towing the jack-up barge Mer d'Iroise, was concerned for the safety of the six men on the barge in a north-easterly gale and very heavy seas. The stability of the barge, which had four legs, each extending 70ft above deck level, was also questionable. Rotary Service put to sea at 9.45pm, under the command of Coxswain Arthur West, and headed out at full speed towards the tug and the barge, eight miles east of Lizard Point.

The tug was making about six knots, and heavy seas were repeatedly breaking over the 110ft-long barge. It was pitching heavily, causing the legs to swing through thirty degrees, as Coxswain West manoeuvred the lifeboat towards its port side. On the first run, the lifeboat surfed past the barge and so West had to bring his boat back round again. On the second run, with great skill, West placed the lifeboat alongside the barge amidships, and then held her there. The manoeuvre was made particularly difficult due to the tendency for the lifeboat to surf down the heavy following seas.

THAMES LIFEBOATS

On the instructions of the lifeboat crew, who were standing on the lifeboat's heaving foredeck, five men jumped safely across. The sixth man initially froze, and then jumped, just as the lifeboat moved away. He landed outside the lifeboat's guard rails, between the two vessels, and only the quick reactions of the lifeboat crew saved him from serious injury, as he was pulled to safety before the vessels came together. The lifeboat then headed for Falmouth, where the rescued men were landed.

For his truly outstanding seamanship and tremendous courage, Coxswain Arthur West was awarded a Bronze Medal by the RNLI. Medal Service Certificates were presented to the other lifeboat crew involved in this excellent service, as follows: Assistant Mechanic Ronald Twydle, John Mitchell, Royston Prynn, Roger Andrew and Alan Barnes.

Although Rotary Service had been sent to Falmouth initially as a relief boat in December 1974, she ended up staying for almost four years, during which time she undertook forty-five services and is credited with saving seventeen lives, including those from the jack-up barge Mer d'Iroise described above. She was not much liked by the Falmouth crew, and the issues with her hull design resulted in her replacement in August 1978 by the USCG-built Waveney 44-001. She was then taken to the Fairey Marine boatyard at Cowes, where considerable modifications were made to both the hull and the wheelhouse, and she emerged as almost a new lifeboat. A new steel bow was constructed and fitted, which greatly improved her performance and seakeeping ability, and

▶ Rotary Service on station at Falmouth in the late 1970s.

▲ Rotary Service at Falmouth. Design issues with the boat proved difficult to resolve and the Falmouth crew were not happy with the handling of either Rotary Service or the second Thames, 50-002, which they also experienced when it came to Falmouth on trials. (By courtesy of Falmouth RNLI)

her wheelhouse was also completely modified internally. She was then placed on service at Dover in early October 1979.

Within a month of her arrival at Dover, Rotary Service was formally named and dedicated at a ceremony held in the port's Western Docks on 30 October 1979, to begin almost eighteen years of fine service guarding the Dover Strait, a 'treacherous and violent narrow stretch of sea', according to HM Queen Elizabeth The Queen Mother, speaking at the naming ceremony. Rotary Service is credited with launching an impressive 454 times on service at Dover, and saving 200 lives.

She was initially kept in the old MTB pens in the Eastern Docks, but in 1984, following the development of the harbour with a major expansion to provide new ferry berths which resulted in the demolition of the pens, a new afloat berth was provided in the Western Docks, at the Tug Haven. A building on the adjacent quayside used as workshops by Dover Harbour Board was converted into a shore facility at a cost of £30,000, and Rotary Service operated from here until her withdrawal in the 1990s.

The first services undertaken at Dover came in October 1979, before her naming ceremony, when she helped a surfboarder, a cabin cruiser and a yacht. These types of casualties were typical of the many Rotary

THAMES LIFEBOATS

▶ Rotary Service, on temporary duty at Falmouth, at sea in easterly storm force winds on 19 February 1978, when she stood by the Indian cargo ship State of Kerala for nearly four hours awaiting the arrival of a salvage tug. (By courtesy of the RNLI)

◀ Rotary Service on trials in 1979 having been completely rebuilt, prior to being sent to Dover. (By courtesy of the RNLI)

Service and her volunteer crew aided during her time at Dover. Her first notable service at Dover came on 9 October 1981, when a crew member needed evacuating from the 38,000-ton Danish registered container vessel Dragør Maersk. A force nine south-westerly severe gale, with extremely heavy seas, made conditions too bad for a helicopter to lift the man off so, at 12.15am, Rotary Service slipped her moorings, taking extra crew members with her, making a complement of ten, and headed out to sea under the command of Coxswain Hawkins. Very heavy seas were encountered as the lifeboat made for the rendezvous point, a mile and a half south-west of the South Goodwin Lightvessel. Taking the lifeboat alongside the rolling and pitching vessel was extremely difficult, but Coxswain Hawkins demonstrated great skill as he placed the lifeboat in position at the foot of a pilot hoist on the vessel's port side, with Second Coxswain Roy Couzens first onto the hoist, followed by Dr Peter Welch, the station's Honorary Medical Adviser, and lifeboatman Garth James, a qualified first-aider. The injured man had

▼ Rotary Service in the MTB pens at Dover's Eastern Docks, April 1984. (Nicholas Leach)

THAMES LIFEBOATS

▶ Rotary Service open to visitors at Dover during the station's annual open day, 11 July 1987. (Nicholas Leach)

a fractured pelvis, so was strapped into a stretcher, and lowered down onto the lifeboat in what was an extremely tricky operation in the dark, with the heavy seas making it dangerous for the crews on both vessels.

Once the injured man and the three men from the lifeboat were back on board, Coxswain Hawkins set course for Dover. During the passage, he had to frequently slow down to reduce the violent motion of the lifeboat. Indeed, as she pounded through mountainous seas, one of the lifeboat crew injured his ankle when he was thrown heavily against the anchor stowage. But they reached Dover safely and the injured seaman was taken to hospital by ambulance. The Master of Dragør Maersk sent a telegram to the lifeboat crew thanking them for their help and the RNLI awarded its Thanks Inscribed on Vellum to Coxswain Hawkins and a special Doctor's Vellum to Dr Peter Welch for this excellent service.

The Great Storm of 1987

The most notable rescue in which Rotary Service was involved took place during the night of 15/16 October 1987, when wind speeds of over 100mph were recorded as the 'Great Storm', one of the most violent weather events on record. There was widespread damage around the country, particularly in the south, with eighteen people being killed. At sea, conditions were absolutely appalling, later described as being of unparalleled severity. Into these terrible conditions, Rotary Service launched and her capabilities were severely tested.

Naming ceremony at Dover October 1979

Rotary Service was named and dedicated at Dover by Her Majesty Queen Elizabeth The Queen Mother on 30 October 1979. The Queen Mother was not only a Patron of the RNLI, but the previous year had been installed as Lord Warden of the Cinque Ports.

Lifeboat supporters from branches and stations throughout south-east England gathered to greet her, undeterred by the drizzle and grey clouds. Members of Rotary Clubs were also out in force as they had provided a substantial part of the cost of the lifeboat, while the Boulogne lifeboat had sailed across the Channel for the ceremony.

Captain Stanley Williams, chairman of Dover branch, welcomed the Queen Mother. D. Imrie Brown, president of Rotary International, Great Britain and Ireland, then presented the lifeboat to the Duke of Atholl, RNLI chairman, on behalf of the 58,000 Rotarians in UK and Ireland. The Duke of Atholl in turn handed over the lifeboat to Captain Peter White, honorary secretary.

Following the service of dedication led by the Bishop of Dover, the Queen Mother formally named the lifeboat. She first thanked Rotary International for funding the lifeboat which would 'maintain the traditions of a service which is admired throughout the world', and she spoke of the fine record of the Dover crew and went on to pay tribute to their families. As the champagne bottle smashed down on the bows of the boat, Coxswain Anthony Hawkins called for three cheers for Her Majesty. Rotary Service then came alongside the harbour wall, and Captain White invited her to board the lifeboat.

▲ HM The Queen Mother boarding Rotary Service following the boat's naming ceremony at Wellington Dock, Dover. Captain Williams presented the Queen Mother with a painting of the new lifeboat at the end of the ceremony.

THAMES LIFEBOATS

The Rotary Clubs fund-raising efforts

Rotary Service cost £199,041, although exactly how this figure was arrived at is dificult to ascertain, as different sources quote different amounts. However, it was largely met from funds raised by Rotary International of Great Britain and Ireland, as well as the legacies of Mary Ann Redgate, Mary Conbrough Fowkes and D.I. Craig.

The involvement of the Rotary Club came about in the late 1960s after Rotarian John Atterton, then RNLI Deputy Director, gave a talk to the Rotary Club of Westminster West (RCWW) about the lifeboat service during the Rotary Year 1967-68. This talk inspired Rotary members to engage in a dialogue with the RNLI to set up a fund in support of a Rotary Lifeboat. The idea gained momentum and there was considerable enthusiasm to fund a new lifeboat.

The Rotary Club of Westminster West (RCWW) arranged a meeting with both the President of Rotary GB&I, Geoffrey Sargeant, and Admiral Sir Wilfred Woods, Chairman of RNLI, on 5 March 1968. The President advised that Rotary GB&I itself could not launch a national appeal, but the RCWW could proceed on its own, so the RCWW set up a Lifeboat Appeal Committee (LAC) to explore the possibilities of raising the funds.

The LAC was Chaired by Herbert Statham and three Trustees were appointed: Herbert Statham, Frank Banfield and John Inglis. Rotarian Roy Lewis of Westminster Pimlico RC was appointed as the Treasurer, while John Atterton was appointed to advise on RNLI matters. The LAC met for the first time on 19 August 1968 and after a number of meetings agreed there should be a 'Rotary Lifeboat' to be named Rotary Service.

In October 1968, a letter from the Club's President appeared in Rotary's Magazine, with a very encouraging response, and the RCWW set about various fund-raising promotions. Tamworth Rotary Club (TRC) had also started fund-raising for a lifeboat, so the TRC joined the RCWW and the appeal was made in the joint names of Westminster West and Tamworth.

More Rotary Clubs supported the RCWW's efforts, and when Rotary Service was built, the boat's appearance generated more impetus toward raising funds to meet its then estimated cost of £200,000. With the assistance of many individual Rotarians and many Rotary Clubs, the total eventually raised was £155,427 and this included an enlarged Rotary GB&I contribution of £84,482. Over the course of the ten years it took to raise the full cost of Rotary Service, hundreds of hours of voluntary service were devoted to a project which brought immense pride to all Rotarians at that time.

▲ Rotary Service at her berth in Dover's Western Docks, August 1990. She operated from this berth from 1984 until her withdrawal in the late 1990s. (Nicholas Leach)

Shortly after 5am on 16 October, Dover Coastguard received a Mayday call from the crew of the 1,600-ton Bahamian-registered bulk carrier Sumnia, which was dragging both her anchors, three and a half miles east of Folkestone. The lifeboat crew had to make their way down to the harbour in total darkness, as the storm had cut the power supply to the area. Inside Dover Harbour, waves up to 20ft high were smashing against the inner face of the Eastern Arm, while outside the Harbour 60ft waves were sweeping over the Admiralty Pier and some stone blocks, weighing fifty tons, were dislodged by the force of the waves. In heavy, driving spray, visibility was nil.

The Dover Harbour tug Deft approached the casualty, which was being driven steadily towards the Admiralty Pier, but in the enormous seas, the crew of the tug radioed that they were unable to put anyone on deck to man a towline and so, at 6am, Second Coxswain/Mechanic Roy Couzens, who was in command as Coxswain Anthony Hawkins was on leave, decided to take the lifeboat nearer to the Western Entrance and wait for further instructions. The lifeboat crew cast off and Rotary Service moved away from her berth, but, as she did so, the wind blew the forward mooring rope into the water which fouled the lifeboat's

▲ A dramatic photograph of Rotary Service in heavy seas off Dover. (David Williams, by courtesy of the RNLI)

starboard propeller. Acting Coxswain Couzens took the lifeboat back to her berth and two divers were summoned who, at considerable personal risk, succeeded in clearing the rope from the propeller shaft, but they were unable to clear it from the propeller itself.

With Sumnia having been driven against the Admiralty Pier, Acting Coxswain Couzens decided to take the lifeboat out, in spite of the rope round the propeller, with Acting Second Coxswain Michael Abbott assisting Couzens on the lifeboat's upper steering position. With the exception of the lifeboat's radio operator, who was strapped into his seat in the wheelhouse, all the other members of the crew were out on deck. As the lifeboat rounded the end of the Prince of Wales Pier, she ran into violent, confused seas, with huge waves repeatedly sweeping over her, soaking the men on deck, who, with lifelines attached, were often up to their waists in water. When they sighted Sumnia, she was hard up against the breakwater, rising and falling 30ft in the huge seas.

◀ Rotary Service leaving the Western Docks at Dover for a publicity event. (By courtesy of the RNLI)

By 7am Acting Coxswain Couzens had, with superb seamanship and great courage, manoeuvred the lifeboat to within 20ft of the casualty's port bow and the lifeboat crew could see two men, each wearing a lifejacket, on the vessel's deck. Fearing that the lifeboat could be crushed between casualty and breakwater, Couzens skilfully brought the boat out stern first and took her round towards Sumnia's starboard bow. Driving spray reduced visibility to almost nil, and at times, although they were only about 20ft away, the lifeboat crew were unable to see the vessel.

As the lifeboat reached the vessel, an enormous wave broke over the casualty and swept the two men off the deck and into the sea. One was spotted about 15ft from Sumnia and, despite a mass of debris floating

◀ Rotary Service heading out of Dover Harbour in heavy seas. (David Williams, by courtesy of the RNLI)

THAMES LIFEBOATS

▲ Rotary Service in heavy seas off Dover. (Barry McGill, by courtesy of the RNLI)

around the ship, Couzens skilfully took the lifeboat to the man. As the lifeboat rolled and pitched violently, lifeboatmen Eric Tanner and Dominic McHugh, with two other crew, pulled the man aboard. The second man was then spotted in the water about 20ft away, and the lifeboat was manoeuvred alongside him and he too was pulled to safety.

By that time, the bow section of Sumnia had been broken off by the force of the huge waves and sunk. The remainder of the vessel was lying on its side, to seaward of the breakwater. Four men were still unaccounted for and Acting Coxswain Couzens realised that they would have to search for them outside the harbour. With seamanship of the highest order, he turned the lifeboat and lined her up for the harbour's Western Entrance. As Rotary Service headed out, she was hit by enormous waves and the full force of the hurricane, dropping 60ft from the crest of one wave and crashing down into the trough, being totally engulfed by the following wave, and knocked over onto her port side. Couzens was thrown violently across the flying bridge as the lifeboat came upright, without capsizing, and quickly brought her under control. The boat cleared the harbour entrance to begin the search for the four missing men. Two harbour launches, George Hammond II and Verity, searched the Outer Harbour, braving the extremely severe conditions.

The crew of the tug Deft then radioed that they had seen a man in

◀ Rotary Service leaving Dover on exercise on 10 September 1983 (top), as a north-westerly gale whips up rough seas. As the lifeboat made her way back to her pen following the exercise, a report was received that the yacht Heathcliff, with a crew of four, was in difficulties east of Dover Harbour. Rotary Service put out again at 1.05pm (middle) and towed the yacht slowly back to the harbour. Once the boats were inside the harbour, the tow was handed over to a harbour launch, and the lifeboat headed back out to sea again to help another yacht, Tomeray, which was in difficulties five miles east of Dover Harbour. As one of the yacht's three crew was suffering from severe seasickness, one of the lifeboat crew, a qualified first-aider, was put aboard the yacht, which was then towed into Dover harbour by the lifeboat at 3.30pm (bottom) and safely berthed. (By courtesy of Jeff Morris)

the water just inside the Eastern Entrance to the Harbour and asked for urgent lifeboat assistance. As Acting Coxswain Couzens turned the lifeboat towards the harbour entrance, Rotary Service was again struck by enormous waves and this time she was knocked over to starboard. Again, she quickly came upright and entered the harbour safely.

In the meantime, the crew of Deft had, somehow, succeeded in hauling the man up out of the water and onto the deck, despite the tug having a freeboard of 4ft. The lifeboat crew then spotted a lifejacket floating in the water, among a mass of debris. With waves still estimated at up to 20ft high, the lifeboat was manoeuvred to the lifejacket and the lifeboat crew reached down to pull it aboard, finding a man beneath it. He was quickly pulled aboard the lifeboat and, although his pulse had stopped and he appeared to be dead, they began resuscitation and he started to breath again. As the lifeboat headed back to her berth to land the survivor, Acting Coxswain Couzens felt pains in his chest.

At 7.27am the lifeboat set out again to resume the search of the Outer Harbour for the two men still missing. Just as the first sweep was completed, Couzens' condition deteriorated, so he asked Acting Second Coxswain Michael Abbott to take the helm as the search continued. Couzens then felt his legs give way and his breathing became difficult, so Abbott decided to rush him ashore as quickly as possible, by when Couzens was unconscious. Because of the damage caused by the storm,

▶ Rotary Service undergoing survey and maintenance at Crescent Marine in Rochester in May 1992. (Paul Russell, by courtesy of George Roberts)

▲ Rotary Service on station at Dover, August 1990. (Nicholas Leach)

most of the roads were blocked and no ambulance could get through to the Docks, so one of the Deputy Launching Authorities took Couzens to hospital in his car, where he was diagnosed to have suffered a heart attack. By this time, the weather had begun to moderate, but the lifeboat continued to stand by until 12.15pm.

For his truly outstanding seamanship, great skill and tremendous courage, Acting Coxswain Roy Couzens was awarded a Silver Medal by the RNLI. Each of the other members of the crew were awarded a Bronze Medal: Acting Second Coxswain Michael Abbott, Geoffrey Buckland, Dominic McHugh, Christopher Ryan, Robert Bruce and Eric Tanner. Shorehelper David Moore received a Letter of Thanks, signed by the Chairman of the RNLI, His Grace The Duke of Atholl, for his help. For their part in the search and rescue operation, the Master and crew of the tug Deft were also sent Letters of Thanks signed by the Duke of Atholl. The crews of the harbour launches George Hammond II and Verity received Letters of Thanks, signed by the Director of the RNLI, Lt Cdr Brian Miles. Letters of Thanks were also sent to the two divers, who cleared the rope from the lifeboat's propeller-shaft, Mr Cook and Mr Gill.

▼ Acting Coxswain Roy Couzens was awarded the RNLI Silver Medal. (By courtesy of the RNLI)

THAMES LIFEBOATS

▲ Rotary Service on exercise at Dover during the 1990s, with the famous White Cliffs forming the backdrop. (By courtesy of Mike Louagie)

Roy Couzens was later presented with the Maud Smith Award which recognises the bravest act of life-saving by any lifeboat crew annually.

Yacht on the Sandettie Bank

Rotary Service continued to be busy at Dover, and on 2 November 1991 was involved in another outstanding rescue. At 6.14pm the sloop Phaedra was reported in distress about fifteen miles east of Dover, near the Sandettié Bank. Three people were on the yacht, but three others had been swept overboard. Rotary Service put to sea within ten minutes of the call and, despite very rough seas and a severe south-westerly gale, headed out at full speed. With Second Coxswain Dennis Bailey and lifeboatman Michael Abbott taking it in turns at the wheel on the lifeboat's flying bridge, Coxswain Hawkins plotted a course to the casualty. At 7.22pm the lifeboat crew began firing white parachute flares as they neared the reported position of the casualty, which, in company with the yacht Donita, had left Ramsgate at 2.30pm bound for Belgium. At 7.44pm the lifeboat crew spotted the yachts, having maintained an average speed of twenty knots during the passage from Dover despite the appalling conditions.

Donita was sailing under a storm jib but Phaedra was being blown towards the Sandettié West Buoy. Coxswain Hawkins approached the casualty stem-first and manoeuvred the lifeboat alongside so that lifeboatman David Pascal could step across. The man on the yacht had a broken collar bone and a fractured wrist, sustained when the yacht suffered a knockdown, which was also when the three people had been washed overboard. A woman on board the yacht was diabetic and was very poorly, while a twelve-year-old boy was shaken but otherwise unhurt.

Once the yacht's crew had been made as comfortable as possible, a light heaving-line was thrown across, and eventually the towline was secured. The boats were just over a mile north-east of the Sandettie Lightvessel, so Coxswain Hawkins decided to make for Dunkirk West, the nearest port. Also, the coast would provide some shelter as they got closer to it. Hawkins drove the lifeboat slowly ahead and the long tow to Dunkirk got under way, David Pascall remaining on the yacht and steering throughout the passage. Conditions on the yacht during the tow were most uncomfortable, with the yacht frequently veering violently down the heavy seas and making steering extremely difficult. At 10.30pm the lifeboat entered the approach channel to Dunkirk West

▼ Rotary Service berthed at Dover in February 1997. (Nicholas Leach)

THAMES LIFEBOATS

Rotary Service in attendance at Walmer lifeboat day in the mid-1990s, together with the 47ft Tyne lifeboat Kenneth Thelwall II (ON.1154) from Ramsgate. (Ray Noble)

Harbour and, with the wind beginning to ease, they were met by the Dunkirk West pilot boat and escorted safely into the harbour. The casualties were then landed and taken to hospital by ambulance.

After a welcome hot drink, the lifeboat crew set out from Dunkirk at midnight, intending to help with the ongoing search for the missing people, but shortly after Rotary Service had left Dunkirk, the French authorities called off the search so Coxswain Hawkins continued towards Dover. With Second Coxswain Bailey at the wheel on the flying bridge, they battled through heavy seas, with winds gusting to over seventy knots, but reached the South Goodwin Lightvessel safely, where Coxswain Hawkins took over the wheel, the lifeboat returning to her berth in the Docks at 2.45am, more than eight hours after setting out.

◀ Rotary Service with Walmer lifeboat, the 37ft 6in Rother class The Hampshire Rose (ON.1024), on exercise with Dover-based cross-Channel hovercraft The Princess Margaret. The volunteer crews worked to take off casualties, with a basket stretcher being taken on board from the hovercraft. (Basil M. Kidd, by courtesy of the RNLI)

For his outstanding seamanship and fine leadership, Coxswain Anthony Hawkins was accorded the Thanks Inscribed on Vellum, as was David Pascall in recognition of his courage, determination and excellent seamanship. The Thanks Inscribed on Vellum was also accoded to Rodney Goldsack for his part in the service, attending to the three people on board the yacht, for whom he was a source of comfort and reassurance. The other members of the lifeboat crew, who worked as a team throughout the long and demanding service, were each presented with Vellum Service Certificates: Second Coxswain/Mechanic Dennis Bailey, Jnr. and lifeboat-

◀ A postcard view of Rotary Service at Dover, with the famous Dover Castle and the old lifeboat house, adjacent to the clock tower to the left, in the background.

▲ Rotary Service, with the new 17m Severn class lifeboat City of London II (ON.1220) that succeeded her, off Dover Harbour in March 1997. ▶

men Geoffrey Buckland, Stephen Pascall, Michael Gimber and Michael Abbot. This fine rescue was just one of many performed by Rotary Service throughout her impressive career at Dover, which saw her save 200 lives and launch 454 times on service.

By the mid-1990s the RNLI had begun the build programme of 17m Severn class lifeboats, which were intended primarily to replace the Aruns, but the two Thames class boats were also soon replaced. In March 1997 a new 17m Severn, City of London II (ON.1220), arrived at Dover and took over from Rotary Service. On 5 April 1997 the old Thames lifeboat arrived at the RNLI Depot at Poole, where she remained until July 1998, when she was sold out of service.

Helmut Schroder of Dunlossit

The second Thames class lifeboat was ordered from Brooke Marine (yard no. SYC 395) in 1974 while work on the first boat was still ongoing and its sea trials were determining the issues with the design that needed rectifying. The two boats had consecutive yard numbers, as they were ordered at the same time, but construction of the second boat did not start until 1974. By then, the first boat had been completed and undergone some sea trials, and the issues with the hull design had become evident.

In October 1974 50-002 was reported to be fifty-two per cent complete, while discussions about how best to finish the boat continued. At a meeting of the RNLI's Boat Committee on 12 November 1974 a paper was presented by Symington MacDonald, the Chief Staff Officer (Technical),

▼ The second Thames class lifeboat 50-002, in her original configuration, on trials off Lowestoft in 1976, flying the flag of Brooke Marine.

THAMES LIFEBOATS

◄ 50-002 on trials off Lowestoft in 1976 prior to the modifications to the boat made in light of the experience with 50-001. At this stage, the boat was to be named Elizabeth Ann and had been allocated to Falmouth.

proposing that the recommendations of the Technical Consultative Committee to reconfigure the boats' hull design be implemented. The proposals would involve constructing a temporary false bow, designed by the National Physical Laboratory (NPL) in Middlesex. The false bow, which would increase the boat's length by between one and two feet and consist of a steelwork frame with bays filled with foam and sheathed with GRP, was intended to give the bow a finer entry into the water. It would be left incomplete with the exception of essential equipment until comparison trials with 50-001 had been carried out.

Quotations had shown that carrying out the modifications full scale on the boat itself would be less costly than if done through a series of model experiments, which had been costed at more than £5,000. Making the structural modifications permanent, as had been recommended by the Technical Consultative Committee, would be quite extensive and be correspondingly costly. As a result, the initial proposal to completely replace the boat's fore end was deemed to be too time-consuming, and so a false bow was added instead to improve performance.

It is not clear when the temporary bow was added to 50-002, but in 1976 the boat was in the water after the initial building work had been completed, and she had began sea trials out of Lowestoft with her original bow configuration. In February 1978 she was taken to the RNLI

Depot at Poole, probably with the temporary bow still in place, and after a month of trials, on 11 March 1978, was sent to Fairey Marine at Cowes for the bow modifications to be made permanent. As discussed on page 33, Fairey Marine were awarded the contract for fitting the permanent steel bow to the boat and fitting out the replacement section as accommodation space. The work took three months, and 50-002 then returned to the RNLI Depot at Poole on 7 June 1978 for further trials.

Hitherto, like 50-001, this second boat had been allocated to Falmouth, and was to be named Elizabeth Ann. However, in August 1978 the RNLI

◀ 50-002 on trials off Littlehampton in the late 1970s, after the bow had been rebuilt and she had been allocated to Islay, to be named Helmut Schroder of Dunlossit. ▼

▶ Helmut Schroder of Dunlossit at the RNLI Depot, Poole in April 1978. The passage to Islay a year later was completed under the supervision of Divisional Inspector Michael Vlasto, with Islay Coxswain Alistair Campbell and Mechanic Archie Campbell among the crew. Divisional Engineer Tom Peebles was also on board. (By courtesy of the RNLI)

decided to reallocate her to Islay and rename her Helmut Schroder of Dunlossit, so the boat never went to Falmouth. However, she did carry out a service under the name Elizabeth Ann, on 22 August 1978, while she was on passage to Dover from the RNLI's Depot at Poole, helping a rubber dinghy before continuing on her passage just before 4pm. It was after this service that she was renamed Helmut Schroder of Dunlossit.

For the remainder of 1978 50-002 was used for trials, and attended the Southampton Boat Show in September 1978, being involved in a helicopter rescue demonstration on 23 September. In October 1978 she was sent to William Osborne's boatyard at Littlehampton for further work, returning to the RNLI's Depot at Poole on 5 April 1979.

Service at Islay

During April 1979 training with the Islay crew was undertaken at Poole, and on 24 April 1979 50-002 left Poole and headed north, arriving at her new station on 28 April 1979. After further crew training at her Scottish station, she was placed on operational service on 2 May 1979, replacing the 47ft Watson Francis W. Wotherspoon of Paisley (ON.951), which had been at the station for twenty years. Her cost, stated to be £200,000, was provided out of a gift to the RNLI from the Schroder Charity Trust, on behalf of Bruno Schroder and Mrs George Mallinckrodt.

▲ Helmut Schroder of Dunlossit makes her debut at Islay in April 1979. She was provided by the Schroder Charity Trust. (By courtesy of the RNLI)

Her naming ceremony was held at Port Askaig on 28 July 1979, and was quite a grand affair, with almost a thousand islanders, visitors and their guests crowded on the pier and harbour. At 5.20pm three maroons were fired and Coxswain Alastair Campbell and his crew brought 50-002 into position just off the ramp of the newly-finished vehicle ferry pier, and the Islay Pipers led branch chairman, Alastair Macrae, and his party to the naming platform. On behalf of Islay branch, Macrae thanked the Schroder Charity Trust for their generosity in funding the new lifeboat and Bruno L. Schroder formally handed over the boat to the RNLI.

Mr Schroder referred to his own enthusiasm and support for Islay lifeboat, which he had inherited from his late father. Their business was

◀ Helmut Schroder of Dunlossit arrives at Islay. The passage saw her leave Poole on 24 April 1979, and call overnight at Newlyn, Rosslare Harbour (a nine-hour passage), Port St Mary and Campbeltown, arriving at Islay on 28 April. (By courtesy of the RNLI)

THAMES LIFEBOATS

◤ Helmut Schroder of Dunlossit makes her debut in the Sound of Islay, off Port Askaig, April 1979. (By courtesy of the RNLI)

banking, but their family originated from Europe and they had always had a close affinity with those who go to sea in ships. Sir Charles McGrigor, Convenor of the Scottish Lifeboat Council, accepted the lifeboat on behalf of the RNLI and, in turn, handed her into the care of the branch, for whom she was accepted by Neil MacMillan. Following a service of dedication conducted by the Rev Ian R. Munro, the lifeboat was christened Helmut Schroder of Dunlossit by Mrs George Mallinckrodt, daughter of the late Helmut Schroder. As soon as the bottle of champagne was broken, the crew brought the boat alongside the pier to embark some of the guests, who were taken for a short trip in the Sound of Islay.

Capsized on service

Helmut Schroder of Dunlossit spent almost eighteen years at Islay, operating from moorings in the small village of Port Askaig, which also hosts the ferry terminal. During a fine career, she launched more than 200 times on service and is credited with saving sixty lives. The most notable incident in which she was involved took place in November 1979, just a few months after she had arrived, giving her crew great confidence in the boat. Late on the evening of 17 November 1979 the Danish cargo vessel Lone Dania got into difficulties six miles north-west of the Skerryvore lighthouse, when her cargo of marble chippings shifted in

▲ Islay lifeboat crew on board Helmut Schroder of Dunlossit; these photos give an impression of the wheelhouse layout of the 50ft Thames. (By courtesy of the RNLI)

very rough seas and a force nine south-westerly gale. Helmut Schroder of Dunlossit left Port Askaig at 12.35am on 18 November and Barra Island lifeboat R.A. Colby Cubbin No.3 (ON.935), a 52ft Barnett class, put to sea twenty minutes later. The wind was steadily increasing in strength and got up to hurricane force twelve, with gusts of up to sixty-five knots being recorded, churning up mountainous seas.

Heading north, the Islay lifeboat ran into the full fury of the storm as she cleared the lee of the island and, at 1.30am, ran into exceptionally large, breaking seas, one wave being estimated at 25ft high. The lifeboat drove through it and then fell into the deep trough behind it. Still they battled on, until, at 1.43am, Coxswain Alastair Campbell suddenly spotted another huge wave, over 30ft high, bearing down on the lifeboat's starboard bow. As it hit the lifeboat, she rolled over to about forty-five degrees to port, hung there momentarily, and then slid down the face of the following huge wave and rolled right over, capsizing to port.

◄ Helmut Schroder of Dunlossit at her regular moorings off Port Askaig; the crew reached her using the small wooden boarding boat. (By courtesy of the RNLI)

THAMES LIFEBOATS

▲ Helmut Schroder of Dunlossit at her regular moorings off Port Askaig, Islay. (Tony Denton)

The lifeboat remained upside down for about five seconds and then righted herself. The engines had both been reduced to idling speed, with the capsize switches activating as intended. Mechanic Archibald Campbell reset both switches as quickly as possible, but it was then found that only the starboard engine was responding properly, and the lifeboat's radar and windscreen wipers were also out of action. Knowing that Barra lifeboat was still on her way to the casualty, Coxswain Campbell decided to return to Port Askaig, on only one engine. The lifeboat arrived back at her station at 3.55am.

Meanwhile, Barra lifeboat was still battling her way out to Lone Dania, which was thirty-seven miles from the lifeboat's base at Castlebay, on the Isle of Barra. At 3.46am, when about eleven miles south-east of Barra Head, R.A. Colby Cubbin No.3 suddenly pitched down by the bow, fell into a deep trough between waves, and began to roll over to port. Looking out of the wheelhouse window, Coxswain/Mechanic John MacNeil saw a huge wave, estimated at 40ft, towering above the lifeboat, appearing as an almost vertical wall of water. Before he had a chance to shout a warning to his colleagues, the lifeboat was swung round quite violently to starboard and capsized to port.

The Barnett, when built, was not self-righting, but she had been fitted with an airbag mounted on her aft cabin to give a once-only righting capability. This airbag inflated as she rolled over, so quickly in fact that the lifeboat actually went through 360 degrees. Water almost completely filled the wheelhouse and the aft cabin, but quickly drained away. Both engines stopped and it was later found that both propellers had

◀ Helmut Schroder of Dunlossit during engine trials off Port Askaig, Islay, August 1996. (Nicholas Leach) ▼

▶ Helmut Schroder of Dunlossit heading away from Port Askaig in the Sound of Islay, August 1996. (Nicholas Leach)

been fouled by ropes which had been swept overboard in the capsize. Coxswain MacNeil checked to make sure that the crew were alright, as four had sustained slight head injuries. The lifeboat's main radio aerials had been swept away, but, fortunately, part of the VHF aerial remained and he was able to inform the Coastguard of the incident.

The Coastguard immediately contacted the Master of the coaster Sapphire, which had also been on her way to Lone Dania, and the coaster altered course and made for the disabled Barra lifeboat. Several other vessels also went to her aid, along with an RAF helicopter from Prestwick, which lifted four of the lifeboat crew off the lifeboat and landed them at Castlebay. Sapphire, with great difficulty in the prevailing conditions, managed to take the lifeboat in tow and, slowly, headed towards Barra Island. Twice the tow line parted, but was reconnected each time. Near Castlebay, the local fishing boat Notre Dame met them to take over and brought the lifeboat into North Bay, where she was berthed at the Pier. Lone Dania eventually reached Castlebay. The double capsize of lifeboats on a dreadful night off Scotland's west coast was a major event, but both had righted successfully and no lives had been lost. Just a decade earlier, lifeboats at Longhope (in 1969) and Fraserburgh (1970) had capsized, but neither had a righting capability and a total of thirteen lifeboatmen lost their lives. Perhaps more significantly, the Thames design had proved its worth, and the RNLI's policy of providing airbags to non-self-righting lifeboats had been vindicated.

In the subsequent investigation into the events, the seas were described as 'diabolical' and Islay's Coxswain stated that the weather was as bad as he had experienced in seventeen years in the lifeboat service. But his and the Islay crew's views of their new Thames class lifeboat were considerably enhanced – it had literally saved their lives – and they realised what a fine rescue craft they had.

Helmut Schroder of Dunlossit was busy during her time at Islay, undertaking about fifteen services a year, although she performed nineteen in 1987 and twenty-two in 1993, but as few as five in 1985. Most of her services were to yachts and fishing boats that needed assistance. On 4 September 1983 she saved six people from the yacht Hydrovane, for which a letter of appreciation, signed by the RNLI's Director, was sent to the Coxswain and crew. On 21 February 1989 she went to the fishing vessel Kings Crusader, of Fraserburgh, launching at 4pm and not returning until 3.30am the next day, saving five people as well as the fishing vessel. Another letter of appreciation was sent to the Coxswain and crew for their considerable efforts during this service.

Another challenging service undertaken by the crew on 18 December 1991, when Helmut Schroder of Dunlossit was called to the assistance of the Russian fish factory ship Kartli. The vessel had suffered engine failure in gale force winds and very rough seas when she was nine miles west of the Rhinns of Islay lighthouse. By the time the lifeboat arrived on scene, the casualty's crew had taken to the liferafts, and together with other ships, helicopters, coastguard and an RAF Nimrod aircraft,

◀ Helmut Schroder of Dunlossit on temporary moorings at Caol Ila, just to the north of Port Askaig, August 1996. (Nicholas Leach)

◀ Helmut Schroder of Dunlossit at her usual moorings off Port Askaig, with the Paps of Jura, the three mountains on the western side of the island of Jura, making a dramatic backdrop.

▼ Rotary Service (with grey hull) passes Helmut Schroder of Dunlossit at the RNLI Depot in Poole in July 1998, as the two boats are together for one last time. The former was departing for Fowey. (Peter Edey)

the lifeboat searched the area until all the crew of the factory ship had been accounted for. In recognition of their efforts, a Collective Framed Letter of Appreciation, signed by the RNLI Chairman, was presented to Coxswain/Mechanic Thomas Johnston, Second Coxswain Alasdair Barker, Assistant Mechanic James Hamilton, Deputy Second Coxswain Iain Spears and lifeboat crew David MacLellan and Michael Stringer.

As with her sister vessel at Dover, the Thames at Islay was replaced in early 1997 by a new 17m Severn class lifeboat. The new boat, named Helmut Schroder of Dunlossit II, took over in February 1997 and the following month 50-002 was taken south to the RNLI's Depot at Poole. She left Islay on 29 March 1997 and called at Howth, Dunmore East, Newlyn and Salcombe on her way to Poole, where she arrived on 2 April 1997.

After service

The two Thames lifeboats were sold out of RNLI service in June 1998. Rotary Service left Dover in March 1997 having been replaced by the 17m Severn class City of London II, and was taken to the RNLI's Depot in Poole. She remained at Poole until her sale in June 1998 to Fowey Harbour Commissioners, the statutory port authority for Fowey Harbour with responsibility for the Fowey Estuary. The Commissioners took over the boat during July 1998 and she left Poole on 16 July, heading west for her new home.

50-001 • Cornwall, Ireland and Lowestoft

After an overnight call at Dartmouth, 50-001 reached Fowey on 17 July 1998, where she was to become a pilot boat. Prior to starting her new career, the

▼ Rotary Service at the RNLI Depot in Poole in September 1997 awaiting disposal after being taken out of service. (Nicholas Leach)

THAMES LIFEBOATS

▲ Escorted by Fowey lifeboat 14m Trent Maurice and Joyce Hardy (ON.1222), Treffry enters Fowey Harbour for the first time; she was in service as a pilot boat there from 1998 to 2006. (Paul Richards)

boat was slipped at Fowey Harbour Commissioners' yard, Brazen Island, in Polruan, repainted and converted to pilot boat standards, before being renamed Treffry and placed into service. On 12 October 1998 she was formally renamed, by Johnathon Treffry, lord of the manor, at a ceremony at the Berrill's Yard pontoon, near Fowey lifeboat station.

During her ten years at Fowey, she was usually moored in the river by the main docks, about 100m up from the car ferry, serving under the auspices of the Harbour Commissioners as the small Cornish port's pilot boat. Approximately 500,000 tonnes of china clay were exported annually through Fowey's deep water harbour, which was also a safe haven to more than 1,500 resident pleasure craft and about 6,000 visiting vessels each year, and Rotary Service acted as pilot boat to assist the china clay cargo ships to their berths.

On 20 July 2005 HRH Duke of Kent, President of the RNLI, visited Fowey and met Fowey lifeboat crew and committee members, as well as harbour staff and school children. He watched an air-sea rescue display and then boarded the Fowey lifeboat Maurice and Joyce Hardy with Coxswain Keith Stuart at the wheel, escorted by Treffry, for a passage to Charlestown. Half way to Charlestown, the lifeboat was called out on a shout, so the Duke and his party were transferred to Treffry in St Austell

◀ Rotary Service, renamed Treffry, moored at Fowey during her days as a pilot boat at the Cornish port. (Martin Fish)

◀ Rotary Service, renamed Treffry, taking part in the RNLI's 175th anniversary celebrations at Poole in June 1999. (Nicholas Leach)

◀ The pilot boat Treffry at work in the Fowey estuary.

▲ Treffry laid up at Bere Island, near Castletownbere, alongside 47ft Tyne Kenneth Thelwall II (ON.1154) in February 2012. (Nicholas Leach)

▶ Treffry laid up at Bere Island, near Castletownbere in south-west Ireland. (Scott Snowling) ▼

◀ Rotary Service, having had her original name restored, at Portland in October 2015, on her way back to Lowestoft. (Neil Roberts)

Bay. During the remainder of the journey the Duke took the helm of Treffry on the flying bridge and brought her into Charlestown.

Although she had a new role as a pilot boat, Treffry's heritage was not forgotten and in June 1999 she was one of many historic lifeboats which assembled at Poole to mark the RNLI's 175th Anniversary, participating in a parade of old and new rescue craft. The boat also took part in the ex lifeboat rallies held at Fowey annually, being involved in the gatherings in June 2003 and again in July 2006. However, by the time of the latter event, Treffry's future lay elsewhere, as in May 2006 she was advertised for sale, and by October she had been sold.

Having been bought by Bere Island Ferries in south-west Ireland, she was sailed to her next home, where she was used as a pilot vessel and

▼ Inside the boatyard at Portland, Rotary Service is prepared for her road journey to Lowestoft under the watchful eyes of her new owner, Scott Snowling.

THAMES LIFEBOATS

▲ After a long journey by road from the south coast to East Anglia, Rotary Service arrived at Lowestoft on 22 October 2015 and was lifted off Malcolm Elvy's low loader at the old Brooke Marine site. (By courtesy of Trevor Snowling)

workboat in Bantry Bay, retaining the name Treffry. She was usually based at Bere Island, opposite Castletownbere on the Beara Peninsula, or at Castletownbere itself, and was worked hard for five years. However, by early 2012 Bere Island Ferries had stopped using the boat as one engine had seized and the other needed repairs, and she was put up for sale. She was showing her age after a hard life and, having been unused for a number of years, faced a bleak future. However, in 2014 a group of lifeboat enthusiasts, led by Scott Snowling in Lowestoft, looked into acquiring the vessel and bringing her back to where she was built, with the aim of restoring her and operating her as a training vessel.

In pursuit of this, the Thames Class Lifeboat Trust was formed in 2014 to raise funds to purchase the vessel and, during the early part of 2015, had raised the impressive sum of £25,000 to buy the boat, thanks in part to a generous donation from Neill Rush, which was made in memory of his late mother, Freda Moira Rush. With the initial finance in place, in early May 2015 Scott and his team visited Ireland, where the boat was out of the water, and began the task of preparing her for the return to Lowestoft, immediately reinstating her original name, Rotary Service.

Getting the boat back to Lowestoft was a major undertaking. The first part of the journey involved having the vessel towed from Bere Island, with the assistance of Souris, a former Canadian Coast Guard 44ft motor lifeboat, first back to Castletownbere for initial preparation, and then on to Portland, Dorset, a journey for which the tug Nomad was employed and which involved a passage of about thirty-six hours. In Portland the boat was lifted out of the water, and a team of volunteers dismantled her masts and upperworks and removed the top of the wheelhouse in order to reduce her overall height in preparation for the road journey.

A few days later, Rotary Service was lifted onto a low loader, operated

▲ Captain Mike Sutherland, former Harbour Master for Fowey Harbour Commissioners, with Scott Snowling at Lowestoft, 24 October 2019.

▲ (top left) Rotary Service at Lowestoft 9 July 2016.

◀ Rotary Service on 25 March 2017. (By courtesy of Scott Snowling)

by the haulier Malcolm Elvy, and a careful navigation of the UK motorway network took her to East Anglia. On 22 October 2015 the boat arrived in Lowestoft, and was taken to Brooke Business Park, which occupies the old Brooke Marine buildings, and thus the boat had been brought to her original birthplace. Once in Lowestoft, volunteers at the Trust, subsequently renamed 50001 Youth Training Trust, set about the restoration work, with the wheelhouse reinstated and the fixtures and fittings removed, to be cleaned and restored or replaced. The intention was to sympathetically refurbish the vessel with modern equipment, fixtures and fittings, while retaining her as close to her original external RNLI appearance as possible, but with a grey superstructure instead of her orange livery to prevent her being mistaken for a serving lifeboat.

Once the refurbishment was complete, it was intended that she would be operated as a youth training vessel, but she was in a poor condition and needed a considerable amount of work to achieve this. Several volunteers worked for many hours on the boat between 2015 and 2021, but difficulties with funding hampered the project, as did finding and installing suitable engines. The original General Motors diesels were unsalvageable, so replacement Scania engines were sourced.

However, despite Scott's considerable efforts and dedication, as well as those of the supportive volunteers, when the Covid pandemic struck in early 2020 work on the restoration stopped, and never restarted. With a change in circumstances for Scott, as well as difficulties with obtaining funding, fittings, and new volunteers after Covid, it was announced in July 2022 that, after eight years of hard work, the 50001 Youth Training Trust was being wound up. Dealing with the impact of the pandemic left the Trust struggling, with limited income and a reduction in volunteer availability.

Trying to get the work carried out professionally proved difficult, with verbal estimates of approximately £300,000 to complete Rotary Service, but no written quotations, which were needed in order to seek grant funding. With grant funding not available, the trustees felt that the project was no longer financially viable. As a result the boat was offered for sale during the second half of 2022, having been stripped of all fixtures and fittings. Many original parts were included, but there were no electronics, pipework or machinery, including engines. As of December 2023 the boat remains for sale, but faces an uncertain future.

◀ The old Brooke Marine site at Lowestoft where Rotary Service has remained since 2015; she is pictured on 3 June 2018 with restoraton work ongoing. (Nicholas Leach)

◀ Restoration work at a standstill, Rotary Service pictured at Lowestoft on 13 August 2022 and facing a somewhat uncertain future. (Nicholas Leach)

THAMES LIFEBOATS

50-002 • New Zealand

After being replaced at Islay in March 1997, 50-002 left Port Askaig on 29 March 1997 and was taken south to the RNLI Depot at Poole, calling at Howth, Dunmore East, Newlyn and Salcombe on her passage. She left Salcombe on 2 April 1997 and reached Poole later the same day. She spent the next sixteen months at Poole, being used for trials, training, and publicity purposes, but never saw operational service again. On 23 June 1998 she was sold to the Sumner Lifeboat Institution of New Zealand.

Sumner Lifeboat Institution, now called Coastguard Sumner, is a voluntary not-for-profit, maritime search and rescue organisation with a history going back to the 1870s. The organisation has operated a series of ex-RNLI lifeboats, and the Thames took over from the 37ft 6in Rother Joseph Day (ex-Diana White, ON.999, built 1973, sold by the RNLI in 1992), covering the sea around Banks Peninsula and Pegasus Bay, near Christchurch, and protecting vessels crossing the treacherous Sumner Bar.

50-002 left the RNLI Depot on 18 August 1998 and was taken to Sheerness overnight, then to Tilbury Docks on 22 August 1998. She was transported to New Zealand free of charge on the container ship Pegasus Bay and arrived in Lyttelton, South Island, on 9 October 1998. She was renamed P&O Nedlloyd Rescue in recognition of the shipping company who provided the free transport, and was formally named and dedicated during Lyttelton Port Company's open day on Sunday 1 November 1998. She then started service as the main Sumner rescue boat, but was found to be too heavy for the slip at Sumner so ended up being based at Lyttelton. There she combined her work as Sumner lifeboat with being chartered to Lyttleton Port Company (LPC), managers of the largest port in South Island, for use as a pilot cutter and workboat

In 2008 50-002 was purchased by LPC and renamed LPC Rescue, but continued as the main rescue boat for the Sumner Lifeboat Institution. She was involved in many rescues, and on one occasion went out more than 100 miles to a casualty. However, by 2010 she was beginning to show her age, and plans were put in place for a faster replacement. In 2011 the 12.5m Sumner class slipway-launched fast response boat entered service, and took over from LPC Rescue as the area's lifeboat. However, 50-002 remains in Lyttelton as an LPC workboat, towing the pile-driving barge around the port when required and towing ships out of the dry-dock.

◀ 50-002 at the RNLI Depot, Poole, on 31 July 1997, having been replaced at Islay just over six months previously. (Nicholas Leach)

◀ 50-002 at the RNLI Depot, Poole, on 4 April 1998, still in operational condition, but soon to be sold. (Nicholas Leach)

◀ 50-002 at Lyttelton, renamed P&O Nedlloyd Rescue, in service as Sumner lifeboat, 9 January 2005. (Gary Markham)

THAMES LIFEBOATS

▶ Helmut Schroder of Dunlossit served with the Sumner Lifeboat Institution as Sumner lifeboat for ten years from 1998 to 2008, having been renamed P&O Nedlloyd Rescue, and was based in Lyttelton. (Winston Churchill Memorial Trust/Derek King archive/RNLI)

▲ Helmut Schroder served with the Sumner Lifeboat Institution until 2008, being renamed LPC Rescue. After being replaced as the lifeboat, she remained at Lyttelton, being operated by the Lyttelton Port Company. ▶

◄ Helmut Schroder of Dunlossit was renamed LPC Rescue in 2008 and was kept in Lyttelton, being used as a work bat and back-up pilot boat. (By courtesy of Chris Rabey)

▲ LPC Rescue retains many of her original RNLI features and has been left largely unaltered in New Zealand.

◄ LPC Rescue on the Lyttelton slipway on 14 November 2023. As well as pilot work, she assists with ships entering and leaving the drydock. (Alan Calvert)

Postscript

The RNLI decided in the late 1970s that no more Thames class lifeboats would be built after the challenging design issues with the first two, but in the early 1980s the situation was revisited. Although the RNLI had, by then, built about fifteen Aruns, and the build programme of the class was ongoing, future all-weather lifeboat construction was being re-examined. An assessment of the relative merits of the Thames and Arun classes was made by Michael Vlasto, then the RNLI's Divisional Inspector Scotland South, and later RNLI Operations Director. Vlasto's area of responsibility included Islay, where the second Thames class had entered service in 1979, and had capsized (and self-righted) on service on 19 November 1979 (see page 64 et seq).

In his report Vlasto stated that the subject was discussed at great length after 50-002 was allocated to Islay, and the merits of the Thames over the Arun for that particular station were grudgingly accepted after a 'hard sell' campaign by both the Divisional Inspector and RNLI Head Office. However, attitudes at Islay changed after the capsize, and

▶ Rotary Service makes her debut at Dover in 1979, in what was her final deck and hull configuration.

◀ 50-001 assisting the fishing vessel Opportunity, which caught fire off Folkestone on 23 September 1994. (By courtesy of the RNLI)

◀ 50-001 at her berth in Dover's Western Docks, July 1997. (Nicholas Leach)

Vlasto stated: 'all discussion ceased and it would now be very difficult to withdraw the Thames from the station'. His views were detailed in a report submitted on 9 February 1981: 'Both classes are excellent offshore lifeboats. Both have similar handling characteristics and virtually the same top speed. Overall the Thames handles slightly better, being much easier to control when running before large seas. . . The Thames is still very much wetter than the Arun, although the latest bow modifications have made it quite acceptable. No doubt if more Thames class boats

▲ Rotary Service in Dover Harbour on 10 September 1983 having gone ot the aid of a couple of yachts in difficulty. (Jeff Morris, by courtesy of the RNLI)

were to be built further modifications could be incorporated in the design to improve [and overcome] this problem.'

He went on to assess the general layout of the two boats: 'the Arun [layout] is considered better than that of the Thames. The open plan wheelhouse/stretcher space in the former being as near to the ideal as one is likely to get in this type of boat. The Thames wheelhouse is cramped and there is insufficient room for all the crew to remain in reasonable comfort for a relatively long period of time, as is necessary for many services off the West Coast of Scotland.'

Commenting on the general performance of the two designs, Vlasto reported: 'I am of the opinion that if an Arun had encountered the same circumstances that 50-002 did in November 1979 it would not have capsized. The reserve buoyancy in the very large wheelhouse structure would have prevented this, allowing it only to be 'knocked down' to about ninety degrees, and then righting very quickly once the freak wave had passed. [But] If the Islay crew had been in an Arun I consider that the injuries they sustained would have been much more severe because of the almost vicious righting movement of these boats. The Thames, with less volume of wheelhouse, was more gentle on the

COMPARISON OF THAMES AND ARUN DESIGNS BY RNLI STAFF IN 1981	
Thames advantages	**Arun advantages**
■ Position of towing post ■ Visibility from wheelhouse ■ Long-term hull strength proven ■ Easier to keep smart in long-term ■ Better for helicopter work ■ Fuel consumption fifteen gallons an hour less ■ Easier to recover casualties from the water ■ Upper steering position less remote from deck ■ Can roll alongside a casualty without much risk of damage to upperworks	■ Better access to machinery and engine room ■ Salvage pump capability ■ General arrangement ■ Better upper steering position although aft deck blind area ■ More reliable and less sophisticated main engine installation ■ Emergency steering arrangements far superior
Taken from RNLI Reference Sheet of 9 February 1981 compiled by Michael Vlasto, the Divisional Inspector for Scotland South (later RNLI Operations Director)	

crew and maybe one should consider that a gentle capsize is preferable to a violent knockdown.' He concluded: 'My personal view is that the Thames class is ideal for stations in my part of the world [Scotland], i.e. Mallaig, Stornoway, etc. It has most of the main advantages of the Arun as compared with other offshore lifeboats and is likely to stand the test of time better mainly because of its steel hull and mode of construction.'

Another report was produced by the RNLI's Deputy Chief of Operations, Commander Mike Woodroffe, on 16 February 1981, comparing his experience of 50-001, which was then at Dover, with the performance of the 52ft Arun on station at Yarmouth, Joy and John Wade (ON.1053). The latter was one of the first Aruns with the wheelhouse layout which became standard on the majority of the boats of the class.

◀ Helmut Schroder of Dunlossit on trials off Littlehampton prior to entering service at Islay, where she was well liked by her crew.

▶ Helmut Schroder of Dunlossit at Islay, after the aft cabin had been fitted with rails for the inflatable Y boat. No provision was made originally for the carriage of a small inflatable, but when the boats were in service a system was developed to enable such a boat to be carried and launched.

His report stated: 'My opinion, based on a limited number of hours spent at sea in varying weather conditions including severe gales in both Thames and Arun class lifeboats, is to favour the Thames, and I consider it to be the best craft the Institution has in the fleet, but that is not to say there is no room for improvement. I consider the faster Thames to have better sea-keeping qualities than the Arun, especially when running before the sea or in a heavy quarter sea and swell. Head to sea, the Thames also handles well, but is considerably wetter than the Arun. The Arun, however, responds more quickly and positively when manoeuvring with engines in a confined area or wishing to maintain station alongside a casualty.

'The current 'operations room' type wheelhouse layout of the Arun is vastly superior to that of the Thames, where the wheelhouse is cramped and I suggest the craft would be greatly improved with larger accommodation in general and wheelhouse in particular. Regrettably, the Thames is still wetter than is desirable when head to sea. The new bow section has lessened this problem but further design is, I believe, necessary to minimise this drawback. The new bow has made for a first class working foredeck.'

In assessing whether more Thames class boats should be built, the pros and cons were listed in a report from the Divisional Inspector for Ireland, dated 6 April 1981: 'The initial dislike of the Thames centred on the layout of 50-001 as a prototype, as well as her reported wetness. The modified version certainly compares with the Arun in layout and reportedly in seaworthiness, so one is left with the following issues.

These are going to be more difficult maintenance issues in GRP in this Division [Ireland], particularly in the remote west. The majority of the boatyards have neither the proper facilities nor experience for working with GRP. The lower profile of the Thames is an advantage so far as windage is concerned, offering less structure to an abnormal breaking sea, and possibly when lying alongside a high-sided casualty. . . The Thames would have the margin [in speed] by a knot or so.'

On 22 June 1981, at a meeting of the Boat Committee, future lifeboat construction was discussed, notably a proposal to construct Thames class lifeboats in lieu of Arun class lifeboats beyond 52-23. The proposal, however, was not approved by the RNLI's Executive Committee, and GRP construction was to be continued. So, despite an apparent preference in many quarters for the Thames class, in the end the RNLI decided not to pursue further construction. Yet the two boats of the class, which gave outstanding service into the 1990s, were well liked at their stations, and perhaps, had the initial development of the Thames been more straightforward, more examples of the class would have been built.

▲ 50-001 and 50-002 together at the RNLI Depot, Poole at the end of their careers.

◄ 50-002 at Poole with the relief 52ft Arun Edith Emilie (ON.1062) on 5 March 1998. This photograph gives a good indication of the design differences between the two classes. The Thames was reportedly slightly faster, and many crews favoured its steel construction over the GRP used for the Arun hulls. However, building lifeboats in GRP was deemed more efficient and economical. (Peter Edey)

THAMES LIFEBOATS

GORE POINT The prototype Thames

What was in effect the prototype for the Thames class lifeboats was a pilot boat built by Brooke Marine at Lowestoft in 1969. The 31gt vessel was completed for the King's Lynn Pilots and went on to have a long and varied career. The initial trials of the vessel showed that she was a good sea boat, but the hull design was slower than required for the proposed lifeboat, so she was fitted out as a pilot boat for the King's Lynn Conservancy Board, and named Gore Point after a headland north-east of Hunstanton on the east side of the Wash.

She had six to eight berths aft for pilots and a couple forward for the crew, as she was initially used to cruise off the Wash, meeting ships and taking pilots off before returning to her base in King's Lynn. When a faster boat became available from Trinity House, she was transferred to the Fowey Trinity House district in Cornwall.

The Fowey pilots, also licensed by Trinity House, had requested an all-weather craft and had a number of boats on trial from Trinity House, until Gore Point was transferred to the ownership of the port's sub-commissioners. A Kings Lynn crew delivered her to Fowey and she became the Cornish port's first all-weather pilot boat. Up until then pilots owned and operated their own open boats. In her early days in Fowey, Gore Point carried the number 1 on her bow.

Based in Polruan, the pilots used Gore Point for boarding and leaving ships and she was moored off Polruan Quay, adjacent to the fairway, on a heavy duty harbour commissioners' mooring. As a result of the Pilotage Act 1988, Gore Point was transferred to the Fowey Harbour Commissioners on 1 October 1988. In May 1991 new Caterpillar engines were fitted, along with new propellers after new pilot boat regulations came into force. A major refit was also carried out.

In April 1998 the Harbour Commissioners purchased Rotary Service from the RNLI and when she entered service six months later, renamed Treffry, Gore Point became the relief cutter. This meant she could work at other ports on a charter basis, and in September 1999 she went to Plymouth while their pilot vessel was in refit. Other charter relief duties were carried out in January 2000, and again in June and September 2002, July 2003 and June 2005.

In 2000 her annual survey confirmed significant corrosion between the aluminium and steel structures, so major repairs were undertaken to the plating and fendering.

In January 2006 the Board decided to sell Gore Point after a replacement cutter had been

▲ Gore Point on the slipway at Polruan, Cornwall.

▲ Gore Point heading out of the Fowey Estuary.

found, and in March 2006 she was bought by Howard Marine, in Plymouth, for £19,250. John Howard had worked on her while she was relieving other pilot boats. After buying her, he used her as a workboat and relief pilot cutter in the port. From Plymouth, after a change of ownership, she went to Eastbourne, where she was renamed Star Gate, and her hull was painted blue and her topsides white. She was then taken to Kent and kept at both Margate and Ramsgate, where she was put up for sale in 2012 through the brokerage firm Boatshed.

By then, she had fallen into disrepair and was at risk of being scrapped. However, J.D. Marine & Sons Ltd decided to purchase the boat and on 23 October 2012 she was lifted onto a low loader and taken to Swansea. Sections of the superstructure had to be removed to reduce her height for the journey by road.

The vessel arrived at Swansea docks on 24 October, where she was lifted off the low loader and set onto keel blocks, and a major refit was started. She was shot blasted back to steel and a thickness test/report carried out on both the hull and superstructure. A large section of the bow stem was cut away and replaced with added steel supports in the fore peak.

The interiors, including the galley, forward store room, fore peak, aft compartment and steering compartment, were cleaned out and painted. Both main engines were serviced and tuned along with a full oil/fuel/air filter change carried out by a Caterpillar engineer. The wheelhouse was completely stripped out and the sections of aluminium superstructure welded back together. All the old electrical boxes, fittings, lights and wiring were removed from all compartments and renewed. The wheelhouse was panelled out with timber, and two new larger windows were fitted to the aft of the wheelhouse to allow for better vision.

Stainless steel wire rope guard rails were fitted, and the top rail was coated in plastic for grip. A harness clip-on safety wire system was added to port and starboard handrails, with independent runners for crew when they were working on deck. A new tyre fender system was fitted all the way around the vessel using galvanized chains, tensioners and shackles.

With the refit complete, Gore Point was lifted back into the water on 11 February 2013 and two days later started a new career as Gore, the port of Neath's pilot boat. MCA Category 3 Certification was awarded to the vessel on 14 February 2013 and, operated by the Neath Port Authority, she was based at Briton Ferry. In 2022 it was reported she had been scrapped after being replaced by Euan D, formerly the Tyne class lifeboat Alexander Coutanche (ON.1157), as the Neath pilot vessel.

▲ Gore Point at Margate renamed Stargate. (C. Lawford)   ▲ Gore Point in service as the River Neath pilot boat.

Thames lifeboats: map of relevant locations

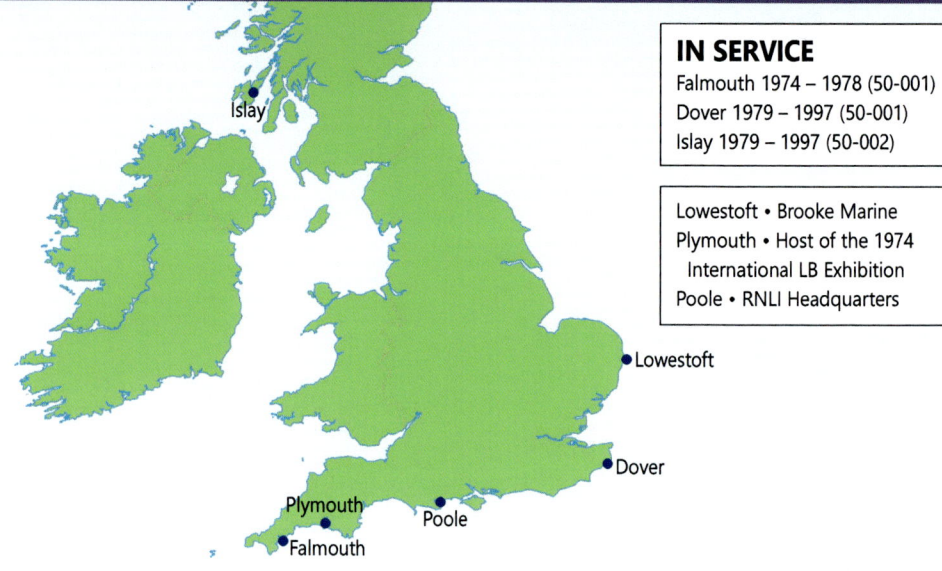

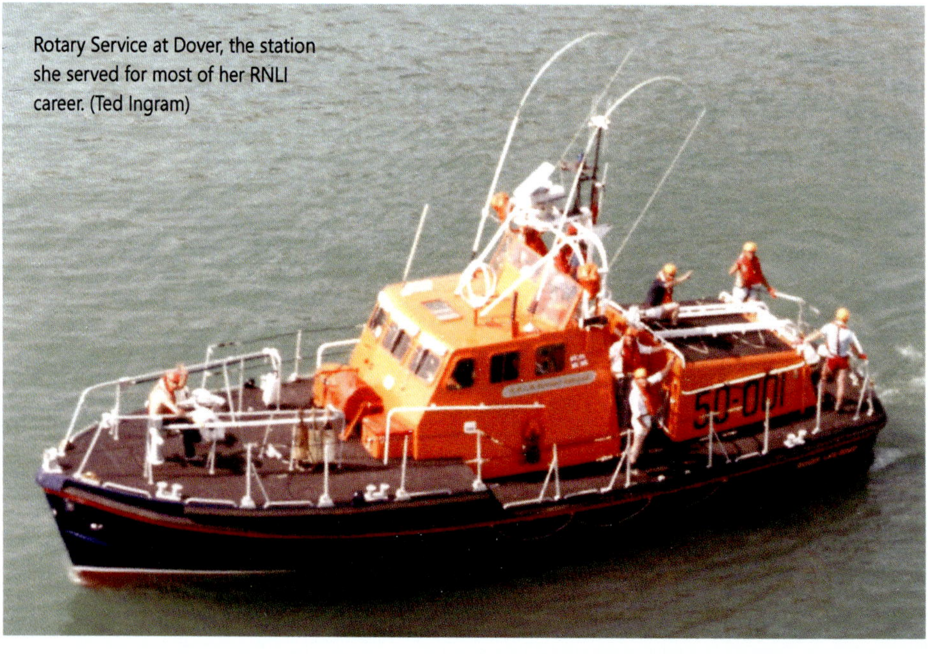

IN SERVICE
Falmouth 1974 – 1978 (50-001)
Dover 1979 – 1997 (50-001)
Islay 1979 – 1997 (50-002)
Lowestoft • Brooke Marine
Plymouth • Host of the 1974 International LB Exhibition
Poole • RNLI Headquarters
Islay
Lowestoft
Dover
Plymouth
Poole
Falmouth

50-001

Rotary Service at Dover, the station she served for most of her RNLI career. (Ted Ingram)